THE CALL TO THE HEIGHTS

THE CALL
TO THE HEIGHTS

*GUIDANCE ON THE PATHWAY
TO SELF-ILLUMINATION*

BY
GEOFFREY HODSON

A QUEST BOOK

Published under a grant from the Kern Foundation

THE THEOSOPHICAL PUBLISHING HOUSE
Wheaton, Ill., U.S.A.
Madras, India/London, England

³|₀³

First Quest Edition published by the Theosophical Publishing House, Wheaton, Illinois, a department of The Theosophical Society in America, 1975

Library of Congress Cataloging in Publication Data

Hodson, Geoffrey.
    The call to the heights.

    (A Quest book)
    Includes index.
    1. Theosophy. 2. Spiritual Life. I. Title.
BP565.H635C3   248' .2   75-30656
ISBN 0-8356-0477-2

Printed in the United States of America

gift

The contents of this book are largely derived
from a study of ancient, medieval, and modern literature
upon the subject of the spiritual life.

ACKNOWLEDGMENTS

My profound gratitude is here offered to my wife, Sandra, who took down at my dictation the whole of this book, typed the first manuscript, and assisted me in the final editing. I am also deeply indebted to my valued friends Herman and Henrietta Braakensiek as literary collaborators in this and other works.

v

1

Open Sesame

THIS BOOK IS conceived, written, and published as an offering
to those who are experiencing an inward longing for spiritual
light and truth, and who are seeking a way of living through
which these experiences may find intelligent and useful expression. Such seekers are in revolt against a mode of life that,
in their eyes, appears almost entirely selfish and, in consequence, fruitless. Fortunately there is knowledge to be found
which can lead to a harmonized and intelligently directed
solution of both the general and the individual problems.
Wisdom such as this has always been available to human beings
on earth, though at certain periods difficult to find; for
humanity has passed through very disruptive experiences and
phases of living, both mentally and physically.

In the Greek language, this knowledge is named *Theosophia*,
Divine Wisdom, now known as Theosophy. In Sanskrit it is
called *Brahmavidya*, the Wisdom of Brahma, the Supreme
Deity. When the inmost depths of such knowledge are referred to, it is called *Guptavidya*, the Secret Wisdom. While
Brahmavidya is reasonably intelligible and can prove to be a
source of enlightenment, *Guptavidya* seems at first to be very
mysterious, and those who propound it give the impression of
a strange reserve. Those who discover the Divine Wisdom, the
Wisdom of the Supreme Deity, at any stage of life are fortunate. Still more fortunate are those who find and intuitively
accept the deeper secret knowledge which leads directly to
God-consciousness.

A new world of inquiry, thought, and study then opens
before such awakening ones. They experience an almost pas-

sionate longing for still deeper wisdom, and the opportunity to study and apply it to the processes of living. Sooner or later the earnest and determined student will find himself meta-phorically standing before the entrance to Ali Baba's cave. Some shrink back from what appears to resemble the bare wall of a stony cliff. Disillusioned, as they mistakenly conceive themselves to be, they may turn their backs upon this treasure house and, even with cynicism, resort to those modes of think-ing and living which characterized their preillumined state. Others find their evolutionary stature, awakening intuitive-ness, education, and the example of family and friends urge them to press on determinedly right up to the bare wall of the cliff. Standing there—even if physically recumbent through illness or old age—they prayerfully continue to seek. Such prayers, expressive of their ardent searchings, discovery, and application of Divine Wisdom, then prove to be the "Open Sesame" which will swing wide the door of that cave wherein not worldly but philosophic and spiritual treasures have ever been stored and the supernal Wisdom preserved.[1]

Led by their Karma to enter there,[2] some privileged ones never again emerge into the light of day outside, which for them is now as the darkness of night. In uttermost humility, moved by gratitude, they adopt a meditative posture. With complete abandonment of all pride of mental ability, freed from any limiting and self-blinding preconceptions, they throw themselves open to that spiritual Wisdom by the light of which the cave is illumined. Keenly alive intellectually but with argumentative mentality stilled, they permit themselves to be lighted up and, Ali Baba-like, to become immeasurably en-riched by the jewels of wisdom now revealed to them.

Such seekers have found that knowledge which proves ex-actly to meet their spiritual, philosophical, and material needs. The wisest ones go forth from the cave calling to their fellow-men in their turn to discover and apply to human living that treasure which has proved to be nothing less than Truth itself.

---

1. Karma—The law of cause and effect. See Glossary.

2. In the tale from the *Arabian Nights,* Ali Baba gained entrance to the cave where robbers stored priceless treasures by repeating the phrase "Open Sesame," which he overheard while secretly observing them.

2

The Mystery Schools

ALL SPIRITUALLY awakening persons find themselves confronted with two tasks. These are self-purification and expanding one's consciousness through gaining increasing knowledge of the laws of nature and of human living. In olden days such tasks were carried out during an orderly passage through the classes or grades of a school or college designed for such purposes and known as Mystery Schools. In the beginning the normal entrant progressed somewhat slowly through stages of development, while at the same time carrying out the duties and obligations of a worldly life. He was very well known in the community as he progressed steadily through successive stages of preparation. These consisted of spiritualizing education, or the earlier phases of passage through the grades leading from one degree to its successor. By this means, errors were guarded against and the neophyte carefully guided through the more dangerous phases of occult progress.

The terms *gateway, door, outer court, inner court, temple,* and *Holy of Holies* may well be regarded as part of the Mystery language relating to stages of development and training. These terms were not only descriptive of advancement, but also of states of interior unfoldment or progress by the inner man, the true Self of the proposed initiate.[1] The rite of initiation was conferred only after the candidate had met all the essentials. The fact of being one among a number of others in a Mystery School helped to protect the aspirant against that

1. Initiate, initiation, see Glossary.

greatest of all dangers in the occult life: pride or self-importance over and above other people. This, indeed, is a very grave danger confronting those who seek to quicken their evolutionary development, and the greatest safeguard against it is a natural humility and selfless dedication to the welfare of the human race. In due course the processes of instruction became more and more secret, and the student spent a longer time within the school and less and less time visibly in the world. Eventually he withdrew almost completely into the school. Finally, a successful student virtually disappeared from view, being wholly absorbed in the twin tasks of making further personal progress and helping newer students through earlier stages.

The title of this system, *The Mysteries,* is appropriate for two reasons. First, for a spiritually unawakened person the whole idea of the occult life is a mystery or may even be regarded as ridiculous. Second, the acquirement of additional knowledge, particularly of the laws of Being, bestows added power and so greater responsibility. Secrecy therefore was enjoined as soon as evidence of progress became apparent. For the profane the procedures followed and their associated experiences were mysterious indeed. This was because they were beyond the reach of the mind of the uninitiated and were also zealously guarded against intrusion.

The idea of a mystery is also appropriate for the procedure of elevation and expansion of human awareness, because such experience is somewhat unnatural to man in the present stage of human evolution. Entry into such states prematurely is not without its dangers. In the acquirement of knowledge of the existence of Life-Power as an all-pervasive Presence transcending all familiar limitations of forms, and further of identifying with that Life-Power lies potential harm. The normal concepts and habitual experiences—based on distinctions of many kinds, including enclosed, separated objects—are not perceived, do not exist as far as the ever active Presence is concerned. Furthermore, even one's own self-existence fades away, leaving behind, within the area of human consciousness, only an experience of oneness, mergence within an apparently infinite, form-free ocean. This so completely transcends all customary experiences and states of consciousness that the center of perceiving and thinking can be seriously—if only temporarily—disturbed, even deranged. These are partly or wholly the reasons for the enclosure within complete privacy of all the procedures of what is indeed rightly named *The Mysteries*. These sacred institutions will be more fully considered later in this book.

The gateway to the Mysteries—even if not recognized as such—has become more easily discoverable and more readily opened in modern days. The response by seniors to the inward call for greater knowledge to the end of greater usefulness has ever continued. As the centuries passed and the human mind and spirit displayed evidence of increased evolutionary stature, the method has become somewhat modified. One effect of this modification is that knowledge, earlier guarded zealously, has now become more generally available.[2] Changes from astrology to astronomy and from alchemy to chemistry may be regarded as evidence of these differences.

Those who have eyes to see the gateway and ears to hear the call of the hierophant within find admittance to be more readily achieved than formerly.[3] Nevertheless, the deeper Mysteries will ever continue to be reserved for those true seekers who have become dedicated to the service of their fellowmen. This book of proffered gleanings from the harvesting of others may perhaps also be regarded as an example of these changes. The major purpose for the production of this work is not only to explain and guide those who are honestly seeking and trying to follow a spiritual way of life, but also to assure them that however unusual that life and its governing rules may seem to be, they are in reality perfectly normal, in fact inevitable. All must obey them who in the past, the present, and the future aspire to knowledge and understanding and seek a teacher who will guide them to those benefices.

One practical value of the privileges which follow admission to the Lesser and the Greater Mysteries is that the faculties of abstract intelligence and intuition are thereby greatly increased. This increase is of quite incalculable value, not only personally for the initiate, but for the world at large. Planetary disasters such as wars and personal catastrophies caused by wrong thinking may very justly be diagnosed as inability to

2. The founding of The Theosophical Society in 1875 and the literature it has made available constitute examples of this trend.
3. *Hierophant* (Gr.)—The chief initiate in a temple of the Mysteries. See Glossary.

perceive intuitively the unity of all forms of embodied life. The intimate spiritual relationship which exists between race and race and man and man is normally not realized and even denied in both thought and conduct. At the present stage of human evolution the mental capacity to analyze predominates over the power to synthesize. Human beings fail to consider the whole and therefore tend to act personally, selfishly, and without due regard for the effects of their actions upon others. This includes failure to realize the responsibility of each individual for the evolutionary progress and personal well-being of every other. This failure contributes greatly to the errors of motive and activity from which, under law, all the sorrows of mankind arise.[4]

In these respects, an initiate of the Greater Mysteries emerges from the experience of initiation utterly changed. Thereafter, he knows—not theoretically and not in response to ethical principles alone—that he is not a separated unit as far as the inward reality of his existence is concerned. He realized himself to be wholly and completely part of a blend, a unified totality of the spiritual life of all beings, whether superhuman, human, subhuman, angelic and archangelic. This dramatic and even mentally traumatic experience, changes —completely alters—his idea of his relationship to everyone and everything else. Arising from this, a deepening sense of responsibility for the welfare of all other beings is born and grows within the heart and the mind of one who has been initiated in the temple of the Greater Mysteries. This change is far less in the brain and body of initiates and far more within the inner consciousness, now increasingly guiding the conduct of the outer man. Initiation is an interior experience, an event affecting the inner man, the true Self, rather than the outer person, however physical and ceremonial it may have been.

The resultant change in a person, whether gradual or instantaneous, may justly be described as a transformation. Self-centered, self-seeking persons, indifferent in varying degrees to the welfare of others, pleasure-lovers indifferent to those who are sacrificed to their indulgences—these are eventually enabled to function as sibylline seers.[5] Naturally, such development is far in advance of the normal state of human consciousness and conduct, though there are somewhat rare

4. See *The Kingdom of the Gods,* Geoffrey Hodson.
5. Sibyl—oracular prophetess, as at Delphi and Gumae, for example.

examples of great and true altruists who may justly be described as ahead of their times. Fortunately, their number is increasing in the world, however slightly, and they do exert a spiritualizing influence upon their fellowmen. Unfortunately, both their counsel and example are too often flouted, scorned, ridiculed, and ignored.

All attempts to live and to act altruistically in a largely mental age are met with an almost impassable resistance which must be overcome. The present age may well be described as selfish. This accentuation of self-interest is to a considerable extent forced upon humanity; for the necessities of life, space, shelter, and food must be provided, and this demands intelligent endeavors. Indeed, for the vast majority of human beings, life consists of more or less strenuous efforts to meet pressing personal necessities. Thus, the accent during past and present epochs has been upon one's own self—or egoism.

Initiated members of the Mysteries have outgrown the egoistic attitude toward life, have indeed become powerfully repelled by it. They portray this repulsion toward sensuality and self-centeredness by their modes of living, their self-expression as idealists, philosophers, artists, and practical servers of both their fellowmen and the animal kingdom. Such people may indeed be described as ahead of their times.

3

What Then Is Man?

STUDIED OBJECTIVELY, historical man proves to be strangely dual. Racially and individually he portrays an admixture of ascent to the highest idealism and nobility and also the potentiality of descent into the lowest brutality, selfishness, and evil. As an idealist man rises high above the animal, while in his selfish scheming and heartless brutality, he descends lower than is normal in any known animal.

According to the teachings of the *Brahmavidya* referred to earlier, man is a threefold, immortal, spiritual being incarnated in four mortal, material "bodies." The three parts of man's spiritual nature are reproductions or reflections in him of the Will, the Wisdom, and the Intelligence of the supreme Deity. These three together, in their vesture of light, are named the individuality of man, his spiritual Soul, the Ego in the Causal Body.[1] Both Deity and man are threefold; God the Trinity reproduces himself as the threefold spiritual Self or soul of every man. Man is made in God's image. The poet addresses all mankind when she writes:

> Hurl thou thy cry at Heaven's gate,
> God must admit thee soon or late.
> Thy passport? Saints could ask no more,
> His image at thy very core.[2]

In this spiritual aspect of his nature, man as microcosm is one

---

1. Ego, Causal Body. See Glossary.
2. "Passport" by Angela Morgan.

with the Divine or the macrocosm. The spirit, or Monad,[3] of man is one with that supreme Spirit, who is "unchanging and immortal God, who reignest forever serene above the waterfloods . . ."[4] In Hinduism, this truth is called the royal secret. It is "the one Godhead hidden in all creatures, the inmost Soul of all." The Lord Christ said: "I am in my Father and ye in me, and I in you."[5]

An ancient ritual says: "As God is the center of His Universe so in His reproduction of Himself the center of Man's existence, the Inner Ruler Immortal." The Bhagavad Gita or the Lord's Song states: ". . . And whoso thus discerneth Me in all, and all in Me, I never let him go; nor looseneth he hold upon Me. . . ."[6]

A poet has written:

> All are but parts of one stupendous whole
> Whose body Nature is and God the soul,
> Warms in the sun, refreshes in the breeze
> Glows in the stars and blossoms in the trees.[7]

The Deity, then, is in no sense external to, different or separate from man. God and man are one and indivisible throughout all eternity. This is the one supreme Truth taught in all Mystery Schools and in all religions. In realization of this Truth resides the secret of supreme achievement, power, and peace, for when the individual fully realizes his unity with the Deity, then the power of the cosmos is at his disposal.

The distinction between the Logos of a universe and the Deity in man lies neither in their location nor in their essential nature, but only in the degree in which their triune powers spiritual Will, Wisdom, and Intelligence—are made manifest. In God these are wholly manifested. In man they become manifested in gradually increasing degrees as his evolution proceeds. Ultimately, they will be fully manifest in him as they are now in the Deity. Man is a God-in-the-becoming. This, the ancient sages taught, is his destiny: "Ye shall be perfect even as your Father which is in heaven is perfect."[8] ". . . look inward;

3. Monad, Monad-Ego. See Glossary.
4. *The Liturgy of the Liberal Catholic Church* (London: The St. Alban Press, 1942), p. 132.
5. John 14:20.
6. *Bhagavad Gita,* Sixth Discourse.
7. Alexander Pope.
8. Matt. 5:48.

thou *art* Buddha; become that which you are."[9] In this divine aspect of his nature man is immune from death. The essential man is immortal; only the body dies. Individuality, capacities, character, interests, and affections persist after bodily death. All the faculties attained during earthly life are permanent powers of the threefold inner Self. Neither this spiritual Soul nor any of its developed powers can ever be lost, for they remain in the vesture of the threefold spiritual Self known as the Causal Body.

Now let us consider man's more familiar outer, personal nature. This is fourfold and is sometimes called the personality. This consists of the familiar physical body and three more "bodies" composed of superphysical stuff, rarer and more tenuous than gases, yet with materiality of a kind. These bodies, from the densest to the most rarefied, are:

(a) The physical body composed of physical, solid, liquid and gaseous matter. This is the vehicle of action and self-expression in the physical world, the densest, heaviest instrument of awareness and action.

(b) The vital or etheric body composed of physical-etheric matter, the conserving principle of his physical vital forces and the link between the superphysical and physical bodies. Etheric substance is finer than the gaseous.

(c) The emotional body composed of emotional matter, his vehicle of feeling and desire, finer than the physical ether.

(d) The mental body composed of mental matter, mind-stuff, the vehicle of thought, the most tenuous of the four.

Unlike the Causal Body, these four bodies are subject to death and disintegration.

When conscious solely in this fourfold material and mortal aspect of himself, man is temporarily unaware of both his divine nature and his unity with God. He suffers from spiritual amnesia. As his evolution proceeds, he gradually rediscovers this lost knowledge of oneness with Deity and through THAT with all that lives. This rediscovery of his own divinity and of

9. H. P. Blavatsky, *The Voice of the Silence.*

his unity with God is the immediate object of all spiritual endeavors; especially is it the goal of all who seek the way of mystical illumination, the way of the direct discovery of truth.

The salvation of man from all personal weaknesses, following the so-called Fall, is an ascent into full experience of this fact of his oneness with God, which means ascension into conscious union with the Deity. *Oneness* is the supreme truth; its full and continuous realization the highest attainment of man.

4

The Purpose of Life

WHY IS THE HUMAN spirit incarnate in a physical body? The purpose of man's existence on earth is spiritual, intellectual, cultural, and physical evolution. Eventually for all mankind, Christhood, Buddhahood, or Mahatmaship is attained.[1] These three terms refer to the same state and position on the ladder of evolution which reaches from incarceration in the mineral, awareness as a personality in man, and adeptic powers appertaining to super-humanity. In the world of dimensions, this ladder is a long one, whether regarded in terms of the time required to mount from the lowest to the highest rungs, or in terms of levels and degrees of superphysical awareness (external and interior) to be attained and then passed beyond. All beings have their places upon this ladder of life. Some of them have descended or are descending from supernal heights to deepest depths, while others—human beings among them—are engaged upon the great ascent, or pathway of return to those heights.

The deepest and lowest rung for the present solar and planetary epoch exists, and is very firmly established, in the mineral kingdom of nature. In the plant kingdom, awareness truly dawns. Sunshine with its warmth, and the four seasons with their changing impacts from heat to icy-cold, stir the evolving life from its former mineral imprisonment. Furthermore, the processes of generation in the plant kingdom begin to disturb the inherent life in its hitherto dormant state, espe-

1. *Mahatma* (Sk.) Great Spirit, Adept or initiate of the fifth degree of the Greater Mysteries.

cially where there are flowers. The faintest beginnings of something like pleasure in the animal sense, send ripples over the hitherto smooth surface of the becalmed sea of life. The very first faint and distant beginnings of what will one day become pleasure from sound are experienced. Life, the divine sleeper, begins to dream and in that dream exists the promise of conscious awareness. This means knowledge of that which is external from which later will develop that wondrous marvel, *choice*. While plants do not exhibit this faculty in the deliberate manner which is characteristic of animals and men, certain of them do turn and move to obtain maximum degrees of influence from the sun. The importance of this change from non-choice in the mineral to the dawning of choice in the plant is almost impossible to overestimate; for from this will eventually arise that movement in man which may justly be described as "Godward." Religion in the broadest meaning of the word may be said to have its first faint beginnings in the sun-seeking of the plant; it flowers to God-seeking in man. Man as a conscious being, having passed through the intermediate animal kingdom, begins in full awareness to do what the plant does unconsciously—to seek the "Sun." His religion at first is primitive but rises at last to the practice of yoga, which may be regarded as the highest point thus far reached by life as it evolves through the human kingdom.

The spiritual Self of man is like a seed; it is planted on earth, it puts forth shoots, stems and leaves, and eventually it flowers. As the mature plant is inherent in seeds, so in the Monad of man—the immortal germ within the soul—all potentialities are present from the beginning. Experience brings them out. Every experience is valuable; nothing is wasted, even if it appears so, for silently the seed is developing. It is, as it were, strengthened by the winds of adversity; purified and refined by the rain of sorrow; beautified and expanded by the sunshine of happiness and love. Eventually, man reaches the fully flowered state. Thus, life is educative in the truest sense.

The teaching, indeed the fact in nature, of successive rebirths must here be introduced, however briefly, into this study.[2] The human mind and its physical organ—the brain within the cranium—evolve quite slowly. This applies especially to the physical brain itself. Two major factors may usefully be considered. First, the evolution of the threefold im-

2. See *Reincarnation, Fact or Fallacy?*, Geoffrey Hodson.

mortal Self of man—with its attributes of spiritual will, intuitive wisdom, and abstract intelligence—is continuous. Second, concentrated and persistent pursuit of the ideal of perfection quickens the processes of growth. If continued with complete steadfastness, such a pursuit hastens the achievement of adeptship or perfection through successive initiations.[3]

There comes a time when, in the figurative language of the Mystery Schools, the inner Self brings a particular personality to the gateway of the temple, whether actual as in Egypt, Greece, the East, or Far East, or as a state of consciousness, an attitude toward life. The required rhythmic knock is heard from within, the doors swing open and, led by seniors, the neophyte begins the departure from the worldly life and moves toward the Holy of Holies with its sacred shrine.

The hierophant and assistant officers are already in attendance awaiting the foreknown arrival of the candidate. Whether immediately or after a period of training, the successive rites of initiation begin. Each of these ceremonials greatly increases the influence of spirit over matter until, at the last and final initiation, the dominance is complete. Humanity as a state of being is thereupon left behind and superhumanity is entered.

The goal accomplished, the Adept—contradictory as it may sound—both retreats still more deeply into the depths of his inmost nature, and at the same time outwardly takes on selected modes of action to serve fellow beings at whatever evolutionary stages they may have reached. This may be spiritual, intellectual, or physical, the last being a combination of all three forms of ministration. While the determined adeptic will to attain still greater heights grows in power, so also does that universal love which demands expression in the form of a ministry, in the highest meaning of that word.

In olden days, as already suggested, these evolutionary phases were passed through under the aegis of the Mysteries, Lesser and Greater; for both the spiritual and the so-called worldly lives were then combined. Meditation became almost continuous and was always quite natural. Service, according to the means of expression normal to the newly attained Adept, was continually rendered. In more modern times, retreat within the seclusion of temples and temple-life began gradually to be displaced by various other forms of withdrawal. These were often temporary, the accent being upon the at-

3. Adept, see Glossary.

titude and mode of life. The process of reincarnation and the pursuit of the ideal through successive lives together play an extremely important part in this present day "out-of-the-temple" mode of life.

This is the solution of the problem of the purpose of life, which the *Brahmavidya* or Theosophy shows to be glorious in the extreme. The teaching becomes immediately and physically practical; for once this all-important knowledge of the destiny of man is gained, the intelligent man collaborates. In this cooperation resides the secret of human happiness. The motto of Gladstone expresses this idea: "Be inspired with the belief that life is a great and noble calling; not a mean and gruelling thing that we shuffle through as we can, but an elevated and lofty destiny."

5

The Call to the Heights

FOR LONG AGES bodily life continues in obedience to the custom of providing the necessities for maintaining existence. Increasing comforts, subjective and objective pleasures, love in all its aspects and, of course, the means of obtaining food, all hold a superior place in man's external life and activities.

Gradually, a change occurs. According to temperament, the personal expressions of feeling and thought begin, slowly at first, to become more refined, more deeply psychological and intellectual and—most important—increasingly reciprocal. Self-satisfaction becomes extended to include shared satisfaction. Mental activities, emotional experiences, and their physical expressions begin to be less and less limited to oneself alone. The "other" becomes more important than the self. Sharing becomes the gospel of life, a personal religion. More deeply interior changes are also occurring, are in fact the source of the external alterations in the conduct of life.

The mind, stimulated from within itself, begins to search for understanding, for truth, and for knowledge of the purposes for the existence of all nature and human beings. A logical plan of life becomes an increasing necessity, and from this a personal philosophy begins to develop and be applied to the processes and problems of living. All of these changes are sparked by the unfoldment ceaselessly occurring within the person and, however gradually, affecting thought, feeling, and their expression in bodily behavior. Although unaware, at first, of all that has for long ages been occurring within him, man as a physical person eventually becomes increasingly influenced by and from within his own spiritual Selfhood. Then it is that the psychological and intellectual event is experienced which in this book is named "The Call."

Thus, man is, above all things, an unfolding, growing creation, forever hatching out of the egg-state into a shell-free product like the Great Bird or Godhead. This divine Bird produces, lays, hatches out more and more eggs, perfected human beings. The topmost rung of the ladder of life is invisible to all but those who are most nearly approaching it—spiritually awakened initiates and Adepts. This highest rung may be regarded as virtually immaterial, time-free and space-free, since those who attain to it transcend the limitations of substance, time, and space. The divine nature inherent in all beings has won its freedom from those limitations and is passing beyond the restrictions of matter, time, and space. From such supernal heights a call perpetually sounds forth. This evocatory, interior inspiration resounds perpetually, just as the light from the sun is ever shining. It invites and exalts those able to hear it, causing them to aspire to that self-spiritualization which brings about the extinction of all concept of self or self-distinction from any other. The call to the heights is of immense importance to all beings and, of course, especially to all humans. Subhuman creatures instinctively answer it when, at the risk and even cost of their own lives, they defend and care for their families and those dependent upon them. For man the call inspires intense efforts—if at first only in the material sense—of heroism, self-sacrifice, loyalty, and selfless ministration on behalf of others. The influence of the call upon those able to respond selflessly is to awaken and develop idealism. Thus, from the summits to the depths of the great ladder of life, a power is actively at work inspiring all who are ascending to do so more quickly. Their load may be lightened by relieving themselves of the weight of unspiritual characteristics which thus far have slowed down the speed of their travel.

Physical results are many and various, according to the characteristics of human nature. Some people are moved emotionally, even excitedly, and try from that level to change the world. Emotion by itself, however, is ineffective, is "underpowered," and in consequence many reform movements fail to fulfill their originator's highest hopes. A philosophy of life must be added to the "heart-call" if the movement is to be both effective and enduring.

17

As evolutionary time passes the capacity to hear the inward call and respond to it steadily increases. It is this human development that eventually leads a man or woman to forsake the more human ways and motives for living in order to reach the next rung of the great ladder. At first the willpower to make what seem to be numerous sacrifices of enjoyments and indulgences is not strong enough to produce the great renunciation. Nevertheless, the call sounds forth, the voice chants on, both becoming louder as life follows life in the succession of rebirths. That which at first is conceived as an ideal—imaged from the example of others but more and more deeply known to be the only way for oneself—eventually becomes an impelling necessity. The voice can no longer be ignored, the call no longer disregarded. Thus, moved increasingly from within, changes occur in the character, and the so-called weights and hindrances one by one fall away.[1]

Then according to an unbreakable rule, an outstretched arm helps the aspirant to lift his feet—which still may be dragging—to the next rung above. In the course of time, the period being determined by the inward voice finds outward expression, and the call to discipleship of a Master of Light —audible in many cases—represents and expresses the interior evocation to the heights.

1. *Weights* and *hindrances* are Buddhist terms.

6

The Master's Influence

FROM THE FIRST moment when the mind of a human being turns toward the light of Truth and the bodily person knocks upon the door of the temple, both from within and from without, aid in specialized and perfectly adapted forms becomes available. The door inevitably and assuredly opens, almost as if of itself. The applicant allegorically passes through it, and thereafter the great journey is undertaken, the great pathway trodden.

Further heights beckon. Throughout the whole adventure—which is free from dangers—special instruction, guidance, protection, and empowerment are unfailingly made available to the neophyte. This adeptic guardianship continues until initiation has been achieved and even onward thereafter, until the true royalty of the human spirit shines forth in its fullness as "kingship" is attained. Not only within the mystic and mysterious walls of a temple of the Mysteries, but wherever a truly awakening human being is responding to the call to the heights, similar aid is always available. Such close attention is unfailing given, even if somewhat more diffused or less observable and realizable amid the processes and problems inseparable from life in the outer world.

When a mountaintop has been reached and the health and strength of the mountaineer—mental, psychological and physical—have been preserved, then the dangers and the difficulties associated with the attempt have been overcome. The victorious one then rests in perfect self-protection and command. During the ascent, however, the case is very different. Steep places, including vertical rock-faces; the temporary disappearance of the trail and even doubts of its existence; barriers of rock formations and, on the lower slopes, of vegetation; remoteness from the world of normal living and easily available help; falls and slips—all these can and do assail those mountaineers, whether physically, psychologically, or spiritually, when they attempt to reach heights which tower above the surface of the globe. This is equally true, if not more so, when ascent to the spiritual heights is first attempted. As every precaution is taken against physical and bodily problems certain to confront the physical climber, so also on the pathway to the interior heights, guidance is offered against difficulties. In this case, these are not of terrain only, but of the whole of the aspirant's nature, from the physical to the spiritual, or one may say, of body and soul.

Although neophytes are seldom aware of it, they have long been under paternal observation and the subject of benevolent concern; for it is the responsibility of initiates of a certain degree and also certain Adepts to hold them under watchful care and assist their progress, as far as generally advisable, karma permitting. The adept guardians continuously hold within their consciousness the unfolding higher selves of the whole of the humanity. They note almost instantly when anyone enters the evolutionary phase of spiritual awakening. When this occurs, what may be described as an occult announcement reaches both the adept Brotherhood as a whole and those particular Masters of the Wisdom under whom, by virtue of affinity of ray,[1] the advancing Ego is evolving.

The adeptic response is immediate. Although never intruding unwarrantably, the Master-to-be shares a measure of his own occult power and illumination with the reincarnating Ego of the one whose inner eyes are opening. This is experienced within—sometimes very deeply within—the mind of the man or woman in whom the inward call is being heard. Responses vary, as is quite natural, and these answerings from the inward Self are in their turn also carefully observed. In consequence, the proffered help is adapted with precision to both the condition and the needs of the interior reincarnating Self which is involved.

Thus, the method employed by the Master and the experi-

---

1. Ray—One of seven cosmic influences reflected throughout nature and in seven basic human temperaments.

ences passed through by the pupil vary according to circumstances—bodily, emotional, mental, environmental, and of course karmic; for the Master is ruled by these in his approach to the prospective pupil and his choice of method throughout the periods known as probation and accepted discipleship. With perfected wisdom, that influence and that guidance which will be most effective at each stage of development, are made available to the awakening human soul and its personality. This occult ministration may result in mystical experiences, periods of spiritual upliftment, availability of hitherto undiscovered literature concerning the Wisdom Religion, inspiring dreams, and a general intensification of the burgeoning idealism.

When the time is judged to be ripe, helpful influence upon the physical waking life of the recipient is brought about. In some cases this ministration is not performed very impressively at first, lest the recipient should feel moved to be on guard. The preservation of absolute freedom on the part of the awakening one is all-important. Aid may seem to be almost casual. Indeed, it *is* experimental, since it is not possible in the early stages of such development to foretell how the "intrusion" will be received. Nevertheless, guidance is at this point proffered to every genuine seeker in both the material and the spiritual aspects of life. A messenger—whether conscious of the mission or not—arrives and offers helpful guidance and support. Strangers, friends, old and new; a touch on the arm, apparently somewhat light-hearted; the gift of literature appropriate to the temperament; and perhaps the drawing of attention to a philosophic movement in which the growing idealism is already being expressed may be the first apparently external signs by which the aspirant becomes aware that his interior change has beeen observed. The guidance is repeated in order that apparently accidental offerings of help should never be ignored or allowed to pass by without careful examination, particularly of the prospects for needed help that such offers contain. All these come under the notice and attract the attention and interest of those who are moving away from the pursuit of purely physical pleasures, desirable and undesirable.

These preliminary adeptic responses to reactions to the call to the heights, followed by the inward and outward search, casual though at times they may seem are, in fact, of supreme importance. On some occasions crucial issues are involved in such early encounters and, in their continuance and development when responses prove favorable, unforeseen and indeed unpredictable changes of circumstance may follow. Indeed, looking back later in life, the first reception of guidance—and of course the guidance itself—is seen to be of extreme significance. The moment can be critical. All seekers are therefore strongly advised never to let a proffered opening into that knowledge or an extended hand be received too lightly or ignored, though, naturally, discrimination must be applied.

At a very wisely chosen period in the life of the aspirant, in order that the spiritual impulse may not die down or be submerged in depressive experiences, a physically visible person will enter his life and proceed to offer counsel for which a need has been experienced. An elder brother appears who will both instruct and, in a measure, take charge of the one who in Buddhist terminology has become *Gotrabhu,* spiritually prepared for initiation, personally and inwardly evolved to a sufficient degree. A hand is metaphorically held out and grasps that of the awakened person, and when he is willing, leads him toward the gateway of the Mysteries. Thus, direct physical assistance is always available, whether accepted or not, to every single person who genuinely seeks to achieve a quickening of evolution in order to be more effective as an agent in charitable works, in the largest meaning of that word. By selflessness of motive they prove worthy of personal aid and are likely to respond favorably. In some cases a teacher, a guide, philosopher and friend appears almost miraculously in their lives. The neophyte is thus counseled to make careful observation of, and discrimination toward people who—even apparently by accident—come into his life. The likelihood exists that among them may be that guide, philosopher, and friend who is most needed and likely to be most helpful at the time. Such an arrival on the scene of a person's life of the needed spiritual counselor is an event of very great, if not crucial, importance. Karma, of course, plays its significant part in such conditions as the manner of meeting. Under favorable circumstances, this encounter is unmistakable, the newcomer frankly and definitely declaring himself or herself and giving the reason for arrival and the proffered help. In such a case, acceptance of that guidance is gratefully expressed and the relationship between teacher and pupil becomes established, continues, and leads on until that pupil becomes teacher in his or her turn.

Past services having been rendered in earlier lives and in the present incarnation, karma permits, even brings about, harmonious relationships, mental and spiritual receptiveness between teacher and the one taught. Steady progress is then made toward self-discovery and the perception of Truth. Other aspirants toward the spiritual heights—temperament here being admittedly involved—may not only accept but actively seek external aid. When the motive is to benefit the world, this quest is always rewarded.

In this a law of the inner life is being obeyed, as indeed is imperative since the law brooks neither denial nor delay. Just as the Master Jesus the Christ entered the lives of his disciples-to-be and called them to the heights, so also in every land and on every occasion teachers of varying degree of spiritual and occult advancement enter the life of the aspirant. Thus a principle from which no deviation can occur is found to govern both the early experiences of a decisively moved aspirant and the responses by the Adept destined to become his Master. Though phases through which the human mind, heart, and conditions of life pass can be diverse and even difficult, wisely given adeptic aid is assured from the very first. There will inevitably be tests, since every aspiring person must find sufficient strength to stand and move forward on his own feet. Nevertheless, interior and external guidance is always available to the resolute idealist. Wise seekers, catching sight of these signposts, stop to read and to learn of the direction to which they point. Contemplation and association with others similarly moved can halt footsteps that lead to the temporal worldly life and reverse them. In consequence, the ancient pathway is found and trodden that leads from the impermanent to the permanent, from the transient to the ever-enduring, from the unreal to the Real. In the successful aspirants intuitive and intellectual responses are sufficiently favorable to permit taking the next steps. These are succeeded in due course—and at a time chosen with adeptic wisdom and skill—by the definite entry of the Master upon the consciousness and life of the aspirant. Then the original friend may or may not remain within immediate reach.

Ceremonials, ancient and modern, have been designed by the guardians of the race—members of the Brotherhood of Adepts—as means to hasten seekers along the upward way. The ancient Mysteries—the Lesser and the Greater—were

23

designed for these very purposes. Initiates from olden times, members of the ancient rites who have not yet achieved freedom from the wheel of birth and death, reincarnate and again seek both the mystic path and the Mystery Tradition. Thus, throughout the ages, both the human race in general and its more advanced members unfailingly have received and will continue to receive guidance, direction, and guardianship. All sincerely, impersonally seeking individuals and groups dedicated to world service—the decisive factor—are continual recipients of the watchful attention, and on suitable occasions the direct aid, of mankind's Elder Brethren. For those whom it would help, occult stimulation toward the attainment of Self-realization and intuitive knowledge are also made available. No single person, no selflessly moved body of people, is ever without the most benign and most wise, inspiring, and directional benediction. Furthermore, those capable of responding to and enduring the strain inseparable from personal pupilhood of an adept Master will receive that privilege.

7

True and False Teachers

SUPPOSING ONE were admitted into the extremely private life of a practicing, but outwardly busy, teacher of yoga. One would find a certain mental equipoise and a relaxed ease in the management of his or her life. Detachment would also be apparent, both as regards personal success or failure and in the guidance of new aspirants so that they may achieve personal illumination—always the goal. In spite of this external dispassion, however, the teacher will be deeply concerned with the welfare and progress of the pupils and with the attainment of maximum effectiveness in their newly-accepted way of life.

As for the students themselves, two necessities will have to be met from the very beginning. First a thorough understanding must be gained by the pupil of his or her makeup from physical to spiritual, and of the human potential of evolution to adeptship as the Ageless Wisdom teaches. In addition, a reasonably appropriate mode of thinking and living, of belief and practice, must become established in the life of the aspirant.

Thus understood, yoga does not consist only of the adoption of special postures, the chanting of certain mantras,[1] and the turning of the mind to the Divine. While these form the heart of the method, progress depends upon knowledge of man himself, directing his life upon that knowledge, and the eventual harmonization of the interior ideal with the external mode of living. A further aim of the teacher will be to enable the pupil to attain to a state of awareness in which the intrusion upon his consciousness of being embodied is reduced to a

1. Mantra (Sk.) Magically potent chant.

minimum. He does not become physically unconscious, but is so fully aware mentally and spiritually that for the time being the weight of the body and the pressures upon it resulting from posture and clothing are no longer experienced.

A well developed teacher in this field will be able to induce this state in the pupil. In addition, he will elevate the pupil's consciousness degree by degree toward ultimate spiritual awareness. The precise method will be chosen by the teacher as a result of knowledge of the personal characteristics and of probable responses of the pupil, modified by results as the instruction continues. This is of great importance. The choice of precisely correct methods is one of the marks of a true and worthy instructor in both the Sacred Science and the practice of contemplation.[2]

In days of old, as already stated, guidance was received within a temple of the Mysteries. In modern days this attainment is possible through means of one's own efforts alone. Those who prefer to proceed alone are, of course, free to do so, and one can only wish them every success. Actually, such success largely depends upon the discovery and active practice of a suitable form of yoga, whether Eastern or Western, ancient or modern. However, the evolution of matter itself, and so of the substances of which the human brain is composed, proceeds very slowly under normal conditions, particiularly when several lives have been lived without undue mental, yogic, or spiritual effort. Aid from a teacher can reduce the effort demanded and the amount of time needed.

A warning may be appropriate at this point. The openness of the child-state must be balanced with discrimination. Many may appear on the pathway of the awakened one who will proclaim that they are the true messengers for which the aspirant is seeking and that they possess both the power and the authority to initiate and teach. Valid help is available in the form of information contained in *Theosophia* (Divine Wisdom), and the knowledge gained from its study, interpretation, and application to all vital decisions. The painful possibility does exist, however, that aspirants may allow themselves to be misled and deliberately deceived by claimants to occult authority, power, and knowledge when, in fact, the claimants possess none of these.

2. Sacred Science, see Occult Science in Glossary.

Exponents of the Secret Wisdom belong to one of two categories. These may be defined as "the self-less ones" and "the selfish ones." The former, when offering teaching or personal guidance, invariably seek nothing for themselves. The latter, moved almost always by selfish motives, seek to entangle their audiences and recipients of their interest within a very subtle skein of proclaimed authority and forms of so-called divine inspiration. A glamor may be cast upon the mind by their specious suggestions and invitations, in most of which a personal element will be discernible. This may take the forms of maneuvers to gain accepted sponsorship, to draw people into membership of their pretended occult groups, and of exhibitions of personal and even physically pretended affection. Such leaders are desirous of binding people to themselves and their groups, always for selfish purposes, however subtle.

A meeting with either kind of teacher and the subsequent choice between them provides a test of the degree of intuitive perception which the follower has developed. However, in addition to a warning, guidance may also be offered. The personal element and clear evidence of various forms of desire for recognition, may serve as unfailing indications of unworthiness and even of evil designs. Beware of all those whose outstanding characteristic consists of "self-proclamation."

In some there exists that strange quality of character which causes them to experience a subtle delight in leading aspirants astray. Particularly, they take pleasure in destroying accepted ideals and personal associations with "guides, philosophers and friends." This is a very dangerous group of people who are responsible for grave injury to spiritual aspirants, especially those newly embarked upon the great quest. It is well to be warned about them and to be on guard against their Machiavellian purposes and methods; the search for truth and its expression in daily living may be marred, misdirected, and even defeated for the remainder of an incarnation.

Just as there are orders of intelligences such as archangels, high initiates, and Adepts, whose whole purpose for existence is to collaborate with the evolutionary procedures—both universal and on earth—so also, their antitheses exist, whose motives are oppositely directed. They use as agents those who seek to defraud and misdirect beginners approaching the steep and narrow way. Diabolically instructed and impelled by them, sometimes even without being fully aware of the fact, these agents constitute a further potential ensnarement. They 27 may themselves be under probation on the path, thus far having failed very signally, fallen victims to the allurements of gratified pride, prestige, and even worldly wealth. When such ones have been met and unmasked, not only should all future entanglements with their pernicious personalities and methods be avoided, but others similarly seeking for truth may well be guarded and warned against becoming entrapped by fair-seeming offerings and promises. The selfless ones ask nothing in return for their offerings of help. They will neither ask nor accept any return which has the slightest taint of personal satisfaction or acquisition. Indeed, it is with some difficulty that they may be persuaded to receive any gifts other than those given out of sincere and profound gratitude, or which courtesy demands should be accepted.

True teachers will have evolved beyond making any personal claims of spiritual attainment and occult authority and shrink from the slightest indication that they are unusual people. Their approach may be friendly but always impersonal. They place themselves side by side with the seeker for truth giving the impression that they are traveling together along the same road. They make no claims for inerrant exactitude, leaving their hearers free to formulate their own ideas, especially concerning acceptance or questioning of teachings. In addition, they will never seek to bind a student to themselves or an organization for which they are responsible. Indeed, freedom is the keynote of both their gospel and their method of presenting it. It is particularly characterized by the absence of all attempt to persuade anyone to embark upon the difficult ascent. They know by experience that the upward path is inescapably the source of much strain, if not pain. Everyone who approaches even the gateway and the outer court of the temple of the Mysteries must ever be on guard. This may prove difficult; for sheer mental and physical fatigue—producing lowered instinctual watchfulness—may lead to an overready and even precipitate acceptance of the proffered guiding hand, which in fact should properly be described as a talon.

The acid test that infallibly reveals the personal nature, the motive and the conduct of life, may be described by means of two words whose meaning is diametrically opposed. These are *give* and *gain*. The truly selfless aspirants to discipleship and all that may be beyond, seek only to give and are contented only by giving. The selfish ones, on the other hand, seek only personal gain and their satisfaction comes from getting. In both cases, the motive may be either naturally or deliberately withheld from public view. The true giver gives for love's sake and abhors the remotest idea of service for reward, and still more a selfishness which is hypocritically concealed under an idealistic guise. Not so the counterpart who, with an expression of smiling love, is forever plotting recompense, whether mental, emotional, material, or all three.

In the former case, the "bloom" opens naturally to reveal an ever-increasing immortal and transcendent beauty, fragrance, and deathlessness or immortality.[3] In the latter, the self-driven, gain-getting human beings become characterized by an increasing darkness, repulsiveness and ugliness which emerge from within the twisted heart of those whose god is self. Awakening and awakened seekers for light and truth should wisely follow and emulate the pure-hearted ones whom they will meet and by whom they will be greeted as the ancient pathway opens before them. They must be aware of, and penetrate real motives, however cunningly and smilingly concealed. While these warnings apply to the normally intelligent conduct of human life, they hold special and particular implications and a particular import where the occult life is involved. Once the first step has been taken everything applicable to the normal conduct of one's life takes on a very greatly heightened significance. One reason for this is that correct guidance is of first importance throughout, and can determine success and failure. In addition, a false step can be so disastrous as to cancel the possibilities for occult progress for the rest of that particular life.

No aspirant should ever surrender the faculty of judgment nor give himself in faithfulness without having determined, without question, on which side of the dividing line the teacher stands. Discovering another's motives, whether revealed or hidden, may be regarded as of but limited value in assessing the character of a person not yet spiritually inspired. Prying curiosity concerning the purposes by which an uninspired individual is normally moved may be regarded as an inadmissible fault. On the other hand, there is the possibility of a spiritual relationship, especially that of spiritual instructor, then the most careful, impersonal, and strictly accurate

---

3. *Light on the Path*, Mabel Collins (No. 21 and Commentaries). Theosophical Publishing House, Adyar, Madras, India.

assessment of the character of the individual is completely essential.

Two distinct and very different forms of human inter-relationships thus exist. One concerns the normal together-ness with fellow human beings and the almost infinite varia-tions in such relationships. The other applies only to embarka-tion upon the spiritual life as the only possible mode of living. Then, as aforesaid, the utmost care must be taken in the formation of personal relationships. In addition, motives, words (especially) and deeds—as also outer appearance and learning—can by example and precept produce effects upon the character, standards, and conduct of other aspirants that are out of all proportion to that found in the normal ways of human living. From their first reception, occult privileges carry responsibilities of unusual weight, if only because of the effects upon those drawn into association with occultists. Therefore, in all these respects, the greatest care must be unfailingly observed.

Humility constitutes a crucial test of preparedness for occult instruction and initiation into the Greater Mysteries. None of the world's aspirants throughout all time may avoid this test and its apparently quite natural application. This applies also to those who propose to offer guidance to new inquirers. They too should make sure that no motive of self-gain at any level exists as a shadow of contamination cast upon their character. The true hierophant is ever selfless, notable for humility, and aware of the heights above him.

In all this the conduct of an aspirant may not be controlled by a senior. The responsibility for spiritual progress must rest almost entirely with himself. He must by the very nature of his character, motives, and actions, be left largely alone; for only by secret interior transformation may the further steps be taken beyond the outer court, through the doors of the temple and to that altar before which every neophyte kneels, pro-nounces the required vows, and thereafter passes through the rite of initiation.

If it be asked, as would be both natural and appropriate, when and where such a temple of the Mysteries, an initiatory rite, and an effectively empowered hierophant may be found on earth, the answer would surely, if somewhat mystically, be "these will find the aspirant when once the conditions exist within him and have been given well-adapted expression."

Karma Through Successive Incarnations

AT THE VERY heart and center of existence, pervading the whole manifestation of the divine Idea, there exists one predominant Law. This Law—insofar as it may be comprehended by man—decrees that the tendency to preserve harmonious equilibrium, which the play of universal forces may temporarily disturb—shall always be stronger than the tendencies toward discordance. So powerful and so effective is this tendency that no matter how great the disturbances, how persistent and for how long they may continue, their effects are temporary. The universally operative law causes harmonious equilibrium to be restored in the disequilibrated region.

During the procedures of quelling tendencies to discordance set in motion in earlier phases of divine manifestation, storms of all kinds continue to rage. An example of this is the universal battle between cohesion due to the law of gravity on the one hand and the centrifugal motion of atoms caused by twisting, spinning, and whirling movements on the other. A perpetual war is waged between these two until, as the central point is approached and passed, discordant and separative tendencies lose their power. Harmony—eternal as the principle is—expressed as unified interrelationships then succeeds. Discordance, destructiveness, and flying apart are governed by influences which are but temporary. Father Time, personification of the continuance of ordered movement, reasserts his parental power. In consequence regularity increasingly predominates over disorder throughout the closing periods of the objective expression of the divine Idea. The existence and operation of the law of cause and effect in the lives of men was affirmed by the Lord Christ during his great Galilean utterances, *The Sermon on the Mount.* . . .

> "For verily I say unto you, Till heaven and earth pass, one jot or one tittle shall in no wise pass from the law, till all be fulfilled."
>
> "Judge not, that ye be not judged. For with what judgement ye judge, ye shall be judged: and with what measure ye mete, it shall be measured unto you again."[2]
>
> "Therefore all things whatsoever ye would that men should do to you, do ye even so to them: for this is the law and the prophets."[3]

Examination of a person's surrounding, noting the more salient features of day-by-day events, will reveal to a considerable degree, if perhaps not entirely, the nature of his karmic account. Circumstance is indeed the compelling ruler of a person's life, for it divides restrictions from opportunities for self-expression along chosen lines and by chosen means. No need exists for either a metaphysical or a deeply philosophical consideration of this truth; for quite clearly and obviously, the fulfillment of an ideal—even the gratification of a "dream"—depends upon the direction and control of a person's life by circumstances, interior and external, mental or physical. This applies to everyone, and more particularly to the completely genuine idealist. Circumstances favorable for progress and the time required for attainment largely but not entirely depend upon past lives, and particularly upon successes and failures in preceding incarnations.

The effects of one's personal activities are of very great importance, not only for the present but for the future, when in a following life the same opportunities will become available. Arguments for the doctrine of reincarnation will not be argued here, as acceptance of this process of nature is implicit throughout this work.[4]

The intuitively pursued and intellectually chosen entry upon the path is an important decision. Successive lives will be more intimately linked by the repeated acceptance in each of

1. Matt. 5:18.
2. Matt. 7:1, 2.
3. Matt. 7:12.
4. Reincarnation—human evolution to perfection by means of successive lives here on earth. See *Reincarnation, Fact or Fallacy?*, Geoffrey Hodson.

them of the ideal of the Path. Because of this decision, causes generated at all levels become charged with heightened significance and enhanced effects in both the present and the future incarnations.

As a person experiences the call, mentally and physically, his past rises up and confronts him, especially his conduct in either the present or a former life when this interior change in consciousness came about. His whole attitude with regard to other people, especially those approaching or having reached the same stage, is of immense importance; for karma in an accentuated form then becomes operative. This can not only help, hinder, or completely prevent further progress, but can govern states of happiness or misery for the remainder of that life. At this period in one's life, kindness to all, especially to fellow neophytes, must override all else.

At some point in the great search direct guidance invariably becomes available. That all-important person, the senior friend, appears and with outstretched hand and either whispered or outspoken words, offers the guidance needed for progress along the next portion of that path from illusion to Truth.

The past conduct of the aspirant may, however, not always have been so favorable. This may result in the teacher veiling the truth, which may delay responses or even cause rejection in extreme cases. Aspirants are therefore seriously warned never to fail to accept guidance offered in their philosophical and spiritual studies and searchings. All are advised not to miss an opportunity to either render or receive help in these most important of all activities of mind and heart. Temporary reduction of effort in the great quest, or even withdrawal from it for a time, may bring about failure to recognize one's teacher, listen to his teaching, and act upon the guidance received.

Those who in earlier lives performed all spiritual and moral duties well, whether within or outside the temple, who were faithful to accepted ideals and moral codes, helped many and injured none—such aspirants generated advantages to be received in following reincarnations. These included and still include—for the process continues—being "born in a family of wise yogis,"[5] parents who themselves respond to spiritual and moral idealism and in places where guidance from a guru is bestowed. For the fortunate ones these favorable conditions

5. *The Bhagavad Gita,* 6:42.

remain available into adult life. Karma's decrees may not be denied, however, and even in such a life, difficulties may arise. These very often are created by parental objections, domestic relationship and outlooks, and discordances in the surrounding districts and countrysides. Members of the lineage may demand that a scion of the family choose the profession for which a family has become notable. Apparent "accidents" in childhood and youth; the state of bodily health; unwise response to the demands of human love; surrender to indulgences encouraged by associates and even members of the family; degrading literature; salacious conversations; attractive temptations; the absence of friends with the same ideals—all these constitute grave dangers for the reincarnated occultist. Wealth and power may also delay embarking upon a mode of life in which eventually they must be resisted and finally overcome.

Karma, arising from conduct in former lives, plays a large part in either the ease or the difficulty with which problems may be solved. The kind human being who has shrunk from and reduced to a minimum the infliction of pain upon others will find these problems almost solve themselves. As they arise, pathways leading toward the fulfillment of dawning idealism may open quite naturally while at the same time helpful aid becomes available. The person who has fallen into the grave error of deliberately causing serious suffering to others will inevitably find that pathway difficult to tread and even apparently closed—possibly with a degree of finality for that particular incarnation. Between these two extremes of karmas resulting from former kindness or cruelty, innumerable gradations of ease or difficulty may be found.

Admittedly, these conditions provide useful tests and opportunities for the development of resistance to temptations. Instruction is also received in the less desirable sides of human nature. However, varying difficulties and dangers threaten not only progress, but even the necessarily firm hold upon the ideal of self-regeneration for the benefit of the human race.

In spite of Karma, very little in human nature and experience is ever ultimately and finally fixed. The element of indeterminancy exists in both universe and man. Therefore, an apparently sudden transcendence of normal rules and processes can occur. Thus, an apparently unevolved person may achieve a sudden breakthrough. Evolved individuals —assessed according to the number of lives or achievements in former lives—may be confronted with totally unforeseen difficulties in fully expressing their evolutionary stature and capacities, in a particular situation or goal. Even though they may seen somewhat irrational or unexpected at the time, such experiences have causes, however obscured.

One possibility does exist which, using religious terms, may be described as "spiritual grace." This tends to remain somewhat mysterious, particularly as regards its origin and even its purpose. On occasion, a concatenation of favorable circumstances brings about this often sudden and almost always totally unexpected experience. The very personal benediction of grace could be brought about by such factors as astrological influences; the play of forces in the superphysical levels; the intervention of an Adept or an archangel when the personal karmic situation is favorable. This last factor is sometimes combined with a critical situation in the physical life of the recipient. These conditions may all combine to bring about the experience which is sometimes erroneously described as "a descent of grace"—a mistake indeed, since the contributory agencies and forces all operate from the deeply interior Spirit-Essence, the Monad, which is the Divinity within. The influences and the responses vary greatly, each recipient becoming illumined, guided, strengthened, saved from error by the "touch of grace" in degrees according to temperament and occasion in life.

The condition of the brain and nervous system is one of the chief determining factors in human conduct, and this often depends upon circumstances existing from the moment of birth and afterwards. Injury, however seemingly slight, or favorable or adverse treatment while growing up may play a decisive role. This is notably observable in self-expression at the advanced evolutionary level of discipleship of an adept Master for example. Such factors may also become apparent concerning progress during the practice of contemplation. The element of uncertainty in these and other ways can play part, though the principle of cause and effect will always be found operative, even if not readily discernible.

Unless karma permits and encourages withdrawal into seclusion, the inwardly awakened and spiritually aspiring man or woman must of necessity fulfill all duties connected with hu-

35

man life in the world. This includes personal relations with family and everyone else in one's environment. Whatever the favorable or unfavorable conditions of personal responsibility and duty, in the fullest meaning of that term, these must be accepted. Indeed, neglect of either responsibility or duty at such a time in human life can prove almost disastrous, particularly for that period in which neglect was practiced.

Thus, there emerges a guiding principle, obedience to which is essential to both happiness and progress while traveling the inward pathway leading to the divine Presence. In Sanskrit this principle is called *dharma*.[6] This term has many meanings, but in this sense it may be interpreted as the true, correct, and wisely chosen fulfillment of obligations, or in one English word, *duty*.

Even if the reasonably sensible, right-thinking man tries in every particular to fulfill this ideal, complexities may arise which cause many difficulties. In all this, whether for him the path is easy or difficult to find and to tread, a meticulous fulfillment of existent duties will determine both the conditions and the speed of onward progress. The goal will then become more easily and clearly envisaged, and the call to its attainment will grow in strength until it becomes a completely impelling demand. Passage through so vital a phase of one's inner life necessitates the avoidance of the smallest neglect of responsibilities to others.

The person who in former lives has responded to the call with wisdom and a deep sense of obligation will have a relatively smooth pathway and an increasing freedom from limiting, personal responsibilities. Either in the incarnation in which the inward drive became an inescapable demand, or in one of its successors, a rebirth occurs which provides conditions in which the inward-leading path may be found and trodden to its end with relative ease. Whether only subjectively as a state of mind or in actuality, the ascetic's cell, the ashram,[7] or mountain cave will then be readily available. On the other hand, those who are for the first time experiencing the divine discontent and "the inexpressible longing for the infinite" may or may not find such a possibility of withdrawal from the world easy to arrange. Obstacles may confront them, either subjective or objective, psychological or physical, or indeed a blend of

6. Dharma (Sk.), moral and religious duty.
7. Ashram, a teacher's home in relative seclusion.

both. These can be overcome only in the future by giving prime consideration to the happiness and progress of members of the family and of those most likely to be affected by the conduct of the spiritually awakening person.

The evolutionary stature of the reincarnating Self assumes growing significance when once the spiritual mode of life is undertaken. The very fact that this has occurred—in all those cases where it is quite sincere and inwardly moved, of course—is itself an indication that a certain rung of the evolutionary ladder has been attained; for only a sufficiently advanced Ego can reach and strongly influence thought processes, and with finality decide upon the mode of physical life to be lived. When this stage is entered, the inner Self attains increasing dominance over the outer man, eventually culminating in complete mastery and entire submission. Nothing can finally prevent the ardent seeker for Truth from mounting the symbolic stairway. This ascent leads to revealed, received, and fully comprehended knowledge—*Vidya* in Sanskrit—of the true purposes for the existence of both cosmos and man. An irresistible will is born, grows through youthfulness and eventually becomes a mature, fully unfolded power, increasingly dominating all thought processes. Such will assures ultimate attainment which, strangely perhaps, includes both discovering Truth and becoming that Truth.

The true servant of humanity is one in whom aspiration for the spiritual and material well-being of fellowmen, combined with compassion, becomes the whole purpose for living. He or she becomes the veritable incarnation of these two motives, all else falling steadily into the background. The man or woman whose karma permits the increasingly full expression of these two ideals finds circumstance of great assistance in both material and spiritual life.

9

Entering the Pathway Toward Initiation

WHEN THE EPOCH in egoic evolution is entered and the interior, spiritual impulse—mounting to determination with finality—is experienced, no question, no doubt even, can possibly exist. There may be hesitations partly based upon relationships with others and partly upon the general karmic account such as ill-health. But the quality of irrevocability enters into the situation, so that the question put by Hamlet, "To be or not to be?" is never asked.

Actually, what is normally known as reasoning has no place in the decision. While this may seem unwise judged according to the normal method of making decisions, those who have passed through the experience know very well that the choice arises from levels of human nature and human consciousness deeper than the purely mental—from the spiritual intuition, in fact. The action of the intellect is, therefore, not likely to be called upon. Should this absence of reasoning be regarded as leading to mere folly in the eyes of worldly minded people, the person who forsakes worldliness because inwardly impelled and for the benefit of his or her fellowmen, inevitably earns the opprobrium of "fool."[1] The description of the spiritual aspirant as "a little child" may also fittingly be applied to such an intuitively illumined person.[2]

Aspirants who have heard the spiritual call nearly always

---

1. *Fool.* An occult interpretation of the Tarot card, "The Fool," supports this view. See *The Pictorial Key to the Tarot,* A. E. Waite, University Books, New Hyde Park, New York, U.S.A.
2. See Luke 18:16, 17.

find it difficult either to define or to justify it before those who have not yet had that experience. Its effects may, however, justly be described as follows: an increasingly continuous thought that a new and better way of life must be followed; a recurring idea that however interesting and enjoyable an experience may be when being passed through, it is nevertheless incomplete and so to some extent unsatisfactory; a curious, and at first seemingly illogical, dissatisfaction with a mode of living that is dependent upon externally produced pleasures, especially those of a bodily and sensory character, the mental sensation that someone within is, with increasing frequency, talking to one insistently about the values and joys that do not fade, pleasures which endure and are not dependent upon physical or even mental activities; a deepening will or intention to discover these enduring happinesses, and an intuitive conviction that they are not of the body at all but belong to the deeper Self; the increasing influence over one's mind of such inward conclusions, not only that they *must* be given ever greater place in one's mind and life, but that this is the only existing means of true happiness.

These and other similar unsought and inescapable assurances eventually cease to be intermittent and become continuous. They then become an irrevocable demand taking over one's mental and physical life with a power that cannot be resisted. Others, watching one in whom these changes are occurring, may find him withdrawn as if following some secret train of thought and even temporarily oblivious of physical surroundings and people.

The effect of this interior experience includes a deepening interest in the full nature of human individuals and also a deepening understanding of the forces and causes operating within and upon them. In consequence, knowledge is sought. Literature is read, schools of philosophy are attended. Many hours are spent in silent thought, deep cogitation, and eventually in meditation upon the processes and laws by which universes, planets, and their inhabitants originate and evolve. The demand for knowledge becomes more and more insistent and, in consequence, the scriptures and philosophies of ancient people are studied, notably those from Eastern and Mideastern sources. While the discoveries of modern science arouse an interest, they deal largely with effects and phenomena and thus prove to be less satisfying than those systems of philosophy which deal with the causes, underlying

39

principles, and laws of creation. At the same time, such studies—increasingly demanding as they become—may be accompanied by both flashes and more enduring experiences of intellectual light. The student has begun to tread the pathway which leads to Gnosis, directly and intentionally perceived and fully experienced interior knowledge of spiritual mysteries.

Certain allegorical accounts of the lives of the founders of world faiths may be discovered to refer to Hidden truths. For example, the Lord Shri Krishna, who was miraculously born as a babe in prison under threat of death, is described in terms identical with the Lord Christ, causing him to be named the "Christ of the Hindus." He was attacked by an evil king, as was Christ by Herod, who feared him because of prophecy, and who also killed other male children. Shri Krishna also escaped miraculously into safety and grew up to display divine powers, wisdom, and knowledge. His later entry upon his mission as a Teacher at the Battle of Kurukshetra,[3] for example, and his death as a result of being pierced by an arrow, may be regarded as typical of the mystery story. Shri Krishna also depicted the mystical Presence within, "the Inner Ruler Immortal, seated in the heart of all beings,"[4] as he himself affirms in the Hindu scripture. He, too, was and is acknowledged as an Avatar, a "Descent" or manifestation of the Supreme Deity.

The prophecies and Annunciation of Christ's birth as a human babe; his escape from the threat of death and flight into Egypt; his embarkation upon his mission as a Teacher of men and his performance of miracles; his Transfiguration, Crucifixion, and Ascension—all allegorically portray experiences through which every successful initiate of the Greater Mysteries eventually passes.[5]

The prophecies preceding the birth of the Lord Gautama Buddha; the miraculous events which then took place, his later entry upon his mission as a Teacher of men; his attainment of supreme enlightenment and his death and "ascension" into *Nirvana*[6] are susceptible of interpretation as allegorical. So also

3. *Kurukshetra* (Sk.) The battlefield on which the events occurred that are described in the Hindu Scripture, *The Bhagavad Gita.*
4. *The Bhagavad Gita.* Fifteenth Discourse.
5. See my books, *The Hidden Wisdom in the Holy Bible,* Vols. I, II, III, and *The Christ Life from Nativity to Ascension,* Quest Books, T.P.H., Wheaton.
6. Nirvana—see Glossary.

are the stories of Horus of the Egyptians, Dionysius of the Greeks, and Zoroaster, born amid flames as a manifestation of the very fire of the Godhead.

Such scriptural records as remain and are reasonably accurate, reveal that the teachings given by the Sages to the mass of mankind were surprisingly few and quite similar.

The aspirant may find the company of others similarly seeking, similarly interested, and similarly discovering. The level upon which companionship becomes established is raised from the physical and emotional toward the philosophical and spiritual. Among those thus discovered, one or more may appear with whom an aspirant feels closely attuned and from whom he receives especially helpful guidance. He, in his turn, fulfills a similar service for others.

At this point it may be helpful to envisage, however briefly, the external life of one who has become thus dedicated to the search for truth. Outwardly the ways of life may appear to continue as heretofore. Changes will, nevertheless, be taking place in at least three ways, including the determined purification of one's habits of life, emotional nature, and general mental attitude. Self-discipline, wisely planned and effected, will increasingly displace undesirable indulgences. The pleasures produced by bodily responses which arise from the senses will be reduced to reasonable proportions and in due course disregarded, except where the health and efficiency of the body are concerned. The accent now will be upon the necessity for self-restraint in almost every aspect of daily life. Undesirable habits and customs, heretofore regarded as normal and therefore permissible, must with intelligence be abandoned. This becomes increasingly natural as the grip of the senses upon the mind loosens, and consequently desire begins to fade as a dominating factor in the choice of conduct.

The word *purity* and the condition generally known as *pure* assume new significance. Cleanliness of body, feeling, and thought, and a growing refinement almost automatically become laws of daily living. Purity now becomes associated with selflessness, while selfishly motivated thoughts and deeds and egotistic possessiveness come quite naturally to be regarded as impure. If an inbred and further developed selfishness exists, it would be a complete barrier to both the offer and the acceptance of occult training. It must, therefore, be excised completely. Indeed, the very word *self*, with its more personal

41

implications, not only loses its place of power but increasingly becomes an undesirable thought and word. While personal care and management of the affairs of life must continue and even become more effective as regards health and general well-being, the center of interest moves away from the motive of self-gain toward that of selflessness. The unavoidable necessities accompanying and even controlling man's physical life and conduct inevitably depend upon a measure of self-interest on behalf of one's self and family. Nevertheless, the motive must continually be enlarged to include the whole human race—indeed all sentient creatures—within the concept of, and service to, one's "family." Deeply penetrative self-examination, self-discovery and self-purification are essential if the divine in oneself and in one's fellowmen is to be evoked. As these words imply, success in the hastening of one's spiritual unfoldment and general evolutionary development demands undertaking a mission on behalf of fellowmen. There is a central purpose, spontaneously embarked upon, of elevating oneself above a mode of thought and life which is disproportionately self-centered. The fulfillment of this purpose enables one to become more useful to one's fellowmen. Sooner or later self-interest so greatly declines as almost to disappear, having become merged into interest in the promotion of the welfare of all. Gradually, *this* becomes the overriding ideal, to be increasingly effective in bringing about the betterment of the lot of mankind. This is not forced but becomes increasingly natural, as spiritual idealism becomes more firmly established.

Giving increasingly replaces taking, and generosity wisely expressed becomes an outstanding characteristic of one who has passed through the gateway which opens upon the mystic path every initiate must tread. Heart and hand are open, with mind as the ever watchful guardian, deciding when it would be wiser not to give.

The word which perhaps most simply and directly describes the necessary attitude of mind and consequent conduct is *honesty*. Whatever the connotations of this word may be in public and personal life, for those who have voluntarily decided to tread the path, only the strictest possible application of the implied ideal is permissible. This rests not only on moral grounds—although these should be more than sufficient—but also upon what might be described as the safety of the soul. The dedicated idealist is not only in danger of being discovered in falseness, serious though that undoubtedly would be, but far more serious is the erosion of personal integrity. There is no possible substitute for integrity when once increased rapidity of evolutionary progress has been undertaken and applied to mind, emotions, and the living out of accepted ideals. The ways of the world, the difficulties of human living, the problems of meeting responsibilities to others and the practice of deceitfulness by one's associates in that process, almost *force* a person in his turn to be deceitful; for this takes on the appearance of being the only way in which to succeed. Now, this habit—for such it can become—followed as if it were a necessary practical way of living, can "overlay" the personal mind as if by a dark covering through which the inner Self cannot penetrate. That covering must be removed and this can only be achieved by those suffering from it through meditation upon, full-hearted acceptance of, and the practice of truthfulness. Thus, the aspirant adopts the ideal of strict adherence to truth and sincerity, realizing that in deceiving others he becomes increasingly deceived and self-blinded. Being truthful to others, he embodies truth, and in consequence, becomes responsive to the influence of that higher immortal Man within.[7] Better a thousand times silence than a single, deliberate lie for those who tread the upward-leading, lighted way.

These warnings are not in the least intended either to arouse mental misgivings or hesitations. They are given solely because the very precious quality of deep integrity through and through could be lost by deliberate dishonesty. A person's character could begin to be weakened or undermined by successive surrenders to the unfortunately rather popular self-support that "the end justifies the means." Such a morally enfeebled attitude could become a grave danger, even if only once applied to conduct.

Above all, cruelty or the deliberate infliction of pain upon all others, both human and animal is reduced to a minimum and eventually wholly dispelled from one's way of life.

Harmlessness increasingly displaces hurtfulness, again not only because of acceptance of guidance from others, but from the deepening realization of unity with all sentient creatures. In time compassionate concern for the happiness of fellow

---

7. Immortal Man—the reincarnating spiritual Principle. See Glossary under Ego.

beings makes cruelty impossible. Kindliness becomes the moving spirit, and spontaneous helpfulness becomes dominant in actions and the motives from which they spring.

Normal standards of courtesy, honesty and faithfulness are of very great importance at this critical juncture in the evolution of the soul of man. Wholeheartedness is of the first importance and particularly is its maintenance throughout all that follows.

In addition to determined and persistent self-improvement, he follows the procedures of prayer, attempted communion and experienced union with Deity and with its expressions in the natural objects in the environment. Eventually the organized and scientifically directed practice of yoga—in the full meaning of that term—must be adopted as a consistent part of one's life.[8]

10

Love and Compassion

SANE PERSONS WHO voluntarily enter the discipline of the
spiritual life—difficult to understand though the decision may
be—are actually in advance of the human race from the
evolutionary point of view. There has come to birth and is
already functioning in them an aspect and power of consciousness at which the vast majority of fellow human beings
have not yet arrived. In terms of Western psychology, this is
called *intuition* and in the Ageless Wisdom it is referred to as
Buddhi.[1] One effect of intuitive or Buddhic consciousness
entering into the range of human awareness is to awaken and
increasingly develop the Christlike experience of what can
only be called "heart-breaking compassion." This is deeply felt
for all, especially for all that suffers, human and subhuman as
well. The words of the Lord Christ concerning the Holy City
will exemplify this development of compassion and experiences which then arise.[2] The Jerusalem referred to is not the
Holy City alone, but is symbolic of the whole world of men.

The reason why the disciples of Jesus Christ immediately
"forsook their nets and followed him"[3] is at least threefold,
namely, inward compulsion that cannot be denied, arrival at a
stage of evolutionary growth at which no other mode of life is

1. Buddhí (Sk.) The sixth principle of man, that of intuitive wisdom from
which the faculty of spiritual intuitiveness becomes manifest. See Glossary.
2. Matt. 23:37. "O Jerusalem, Jerusalem, thou that killest the prophets, and
stonest them which are sent unto thee, how often would I have gathered thy
children together, even as a hen gathereth her chickens under her wings, and
ye would not!"
3. Mark 1:18.

possible, and Christlike compassion, increasingly experienced for every pang of pain suffered by every sentient being. People everywhere are seen to be both philosophically ignorant and agonized by self-created suffering under the law of *karma*, as have been millions of human beings throughout the historical era. Compassion deeply moves the aspirant to the adoption of the spiritualized mode of life. An ever-deepening love of his fellowmen makes it quite impossible for him either to decide otherwise or to delay. According to the Hindu scripture, the *Upanishads*, "there is no other way at all to go."

Thus the Holy Grail of intuition is sought not for the sake of its possession as an object and its prideful installment in one's home, but first of all because of an irresistible, inward aspiration that brooks no denial.[4] Secondly, it is sought in order to attain to that empowerment and enlightenment which will increase one's value and one's usefulness to all other living beings. This is the great call, this is the voice which is never still—namely a call to attain to maximum effectiveness as a member of the human race on behalf of one's fellowmen and younger brothers of the animal kingdom. The choice is made to offer the fruits of intuitive wisdom in the service of all the people of the world because of an interior all-impelling supramental decision.

Every Mahatma,[5] every "just man made perfect,"[6] has built into his nature this power of selfless love so that he or she is veritably an incarnation of that divine potency. By inborn love of all living beings and things and a natural tendency to give aid on all occasion, the Adepts lead other inspired ministrants to become exponents of the fundamentals of the Ageless Wisdom. These, also by personal mode of living and by teaching, accentuate the existence of the unity of the indwelling Life. The highest possible expression of this consists of an unfailing—if often impersonal—love for all others. Compas-

---

4. Holy Grail. Here interpreted as a mystical experience from an order associated with the chalice used by Christ at the Last Supper. Idealism included in the chivalric medieval knightly system with its religious, moral, and social code. See *The Idylls of the King,* Tennyson, and the subject of the opera Trisan and Isolde, Richard Wagner.

5. Mahatma (Sk.) Great spirit and Adept, or initiate of the fifth degree of the Greater Mysteries.

6. Heb. 12:23.

sion, humaneness, and simple kindliness are elevated to the most prominent position in the lives of individuals and communities. No man can ever reach the heights of either spiritual unfoldment or personal development so long as cruelty has any place at all in the thought, feeling, and the practice of daily life. Gentleness, tenderness, caring deeply, and active watchfulness over others—especially when they are in danger—these are the ways, however humble, by which the very best in a person's life can shine forth. If the Masters' religion, particularly in its practical expression, were to be described, that description would be *caring deeply for all others*. The evolution of the human race toward the lofty stature of adeptship is dependent upon this attainment. Love, therefore, must become the spiritual, intellectual and bodily ideal, while intelligent subservience to duty governs its external expression.

At this point attention may be drawn to examples of love as the salvation of those who pursue the path of selfishness. There appears a good friend and senior in the inner life, the *Kalyanamitra*,[7] who meets and aids even the dishonest aspirant to the spiritual heights. The aspirant and the *Kalyanamitra*—who is often a Master's agent—may experience a totally nonpossessive and wisely directed form of love which can prove to be of the utmost value. Guidance from a *Kalyanamitra* can be as a lighthouse guiding ships into port over a darkened sea. The office may even be regarded as a safeguard for the person who accepts and fulfills it; for wisely loving service to others may awaken in the server the very highest impulses, motives, and modes of conduct toward the person being helped. Seekers of the lighted way are well advised to become *Kalyanamitras* to wisely chosen recipients.

A further instance of love as a saving power is shown when a person of the opposite sex, for example, wins the love of an individual who deliberately is pursuing the way of self-gain even at the expense of others. The awakening of true love in such a person and its effect upon him or her opens the mind to illumination by interior Self. This enlightenment is capable, not

7. *Kalyanamitra* (Pali). A Buddhist term.

only of saving the selfish one, but of transforming his whole nature. The moral fiber of the newly-discovered loved one is a decisive factor. If he or she is more or less selfish, the lover may choose a similar mode of conduct. A more evolved person already responsive to spiritualizing influences perceives the error in the loved one, and with wisdom and intelligence gradually wins him or her away from deplorable motives and degrading practices. Thus, love may be regarded as potentially the greatest gift which can be either bestowed or received. So potent can such love be that by its magic the heart and mind of a truly wicked person can be cured or saved.

The great Avatars,[8] the God-inspired Teachers and representatives of Deity, the Buddhas and the Christs, who enter the world of men for instruction and redemption, are moved solely by love in the larger meaning of the word. They will endure all, even crucifixion, in order to fulfill their love-inspired mission. Tragedy confronts these Teachers and redeemers of man, in that while the few respond, the many do not. This experience of failure is in no sense due to the absence of the necessary faculty in the Teacher, but always and only to that innate selfishness characteristic of mankind in the present era, correctly named the *Kali Yuga* or dark age.[9] Heroic examples of what may be termed "self-saving" do, however, lighten up the darkened picture. The outstretched hand, words of wisdom and love, knowledge that their welfare is profoundly important to the Teacher can be saving graces for many. If an aspirant disregards the influence and effects of egoic inspiration—conscience, for example—and the love or ministration by an elder, then tragedy does indeed await the deliberately fallen one. However, service given and love bestowed and evoked can be potent to redeem such a fallen one, even from the greatest depths. An inward response to love can prove to be the decisive factor in a resolve to achieve self-elevation out of the mire of exclusive self-seeking. Thus, true and unselfish love is indeed a mighty power, so much so that one is tempted to affirm that love is the mightiest power of all.

Of all the many and tragic darknesses by which human life becomes overshadowed, none perhaps is so pain-producing and so difficult to endure as that which arises from loneliness. To be wholly alone in a world of apparently indifferent fellow

8. Avatar (Sk.) Divine Incarnation. See Glossary.
9. *Kali Yuga* (Sk.) The fourth age of the world.

human beings—this can be as a "crucifixion" indeed. Naturally, as philosophers would say, this experience is self-induced, being the inevitable result of pain-producing conduct of at least a similar character to that of the pain being endured. Human life is law-ruled and one part of the tragedy of suffering is that the true cause or causes are so often entirely unknown to brain consciousness, though never, of course, to that of the reincarnating Ego.

For some people aloneness is purely physical. Family and friends have either passed away or withdrawn, whether mentally, physically, or both. While this is difficult to bear, when it is accompanied by a strange sensation of being mentally alone, isolated, misunderstood or unloved, then the almost continuous pain can indeed be difficult to endure. This experience constitutes one of this world's human tragedies—the sensation and the physical fact of aloneness. However, the experience can be turned to great value—the development of self-dependence, for example, though the sufferer may feel that the price is too heavy.

How can a spiritually awakened one help such a sufferer? He can contribute healing thoughts from his knowledge that no one is ever truly alone. The divine Omnipresence might be presented as one part of the most sublime of all truths. This tells of the existence within all beings and things of that same Omnipresence as an interior and unfailing Divinity. Such a profound verity could be advanced in forms and at times suitable to the frame of mind of the lonely one. If, however, the intellectual approach at first fails to relieve the gloom, then the illumined helper would endeavor to pierce the mental obscurity in which the sufferer is enshrouded by gradually and carefully penetrating the darkened mind with "power-rays" of spiritual light. This latter is, of course, the true solution, since both loneliness and the lightness state which it causes are illusions, however completely factual they seem during periods of acute suffering. Nevertheless, by these two means, a wise counselor would be able to initiate the procedure within the heart and mind of the person in need of the attainment of that Self-illumination which is the only enduring cure of the "disease" from which the lonely recipient is suffering.

The possibility of every attainment, physical, intellectual, and spiritual, resides within that cosmic seed that in this work is referred to as the human Monad. The twists and the turnings on the pathway leading through the self-conscious period of human evolution include the opposite potentialities of darkness and light, selfishness and selflessness, total self-centeredness and universal love. Truly authentic literature concerning Theosophia includes information about self-centeredness and its consequences on the one hand, and selflessness or love on the other. Self-centeredness inevitably leads to total darkness, while selflessness leads to light, to radiance generated in and shining from every motive and deed springing from love. Planes or worlds of existence—both human and divine—that are beyond the distinctions of personal selfhood, by their very nature are atom by atom full of light. Those levels of man's consciousness, however, in which the sense of separated selfhood is dominant are by comparison both dark and dangerous. Passage through these, nevertheless, is found to be lighted and secure according to nature's purposes. In other words, there is light at the end of the tunnel.

The Lord of the universe, the Solar *Logos,* together with choirs and orchestras of angels and archangels, cause to sound forth from the heart of existence the divine theme and all its variations. In terms of human consciousness, these may justly be regarded as proclamations of the beauty and the power of love—the one great theme. The continuous calls for the expression of loving thoughtfulness in every self-chosen deed constitute variations of that theme for mankind.

11

Selflessness

THE MOTIVATIONS for the pursuit of a spiritual way of life may be difficult to define in intellectual terms, as they are intuitionally and instinctively accepted. The overriding reason is the only one that insures failure-proof success and hastened attainment: to help both humanity at large and virtually every human being with whom one comes in contact. A single and well-known word that fittingly describes this purpose is *service*. The more deeply the interior awakening is experienced, the greater is the concern for the happiness of mankind and subhuman beings. This yearning for the general well-being of all that exists grows deeper and more demanding, rendering the aspiring server more and more compassionate. He or she increasingly lives for and within every other individual.

From the first spiritual awakening, through discipleship and initiation in a temple of Mysteries—whether or not made with hands[1]—each stage needs to be accompanied by a deepening sense of responsibility. The absence of this feeling, thought, and intuitively born knowledge of responsibility for the happiness of all others may justly be stated to be at the root of the sorrow by which human life on earth has been plagued. The would-be effective servant, disciple, and initiate must in consequence become deeply moved by a profound sense of personal responsibility. Even for those who are not yet idealists, responsibility is the great need and, unfortunately, the great lack, a deficiency suffered by kings, presidents, statesmen, politicians, and their subjects.

1. 2 Cor. 5:1.

The teachings of the sages throughout the present period of human history have ever included this call to live so that others are helped rather than harmed by one's actions. Here also is the message for today to all mankind. "Take responsibility. Be concerned about the welfare of others, physical, emotional, and mental." This, indeed, is the heart of the religion of the New Age and happily is so becoming for a growing number of idealists during this present period of human history.

The application of this moral principle of actively expressed responsibility for the well-being of others has been deliberately and repeatedly mentioned in this book about idealism. This ideal concerns the fulfillment of aspirations—born of inward awakening—for the hastened unfoldment of wisdom and of progress in the whole human race. The acceptance of the ideal of responsibility will lead toward the sacred sanctuary of the Mystery Temple. However, that progress will be stultified unless this idealism is keenly felt and sincerely applied to the motives and habits of daily living.

The sages, who are conscious of that awakening spirituality from which their own attainment arose, advise avoiding undue self-centeredness, self-concern, and the slightest trace of self-satisfaction, which are poisons to the soul of the aspirant. These all-important foundations must be firmly established, immovably and unshakably built into the nature of the would-be initiate of the Greater Mysteries. Only upon such foundations can success be assured if a human being is to tread the path from human to superhuman levels of evolution to its end in advance of racial time. This is not only a statement of an ideal, but a warning; for as long as the idea of personal benefit remains with regard to the upward-leading path—however unconscious—so long will there be danger of slips and falls to the lower levels, and even of very grievous descent. This could cause aspirants to become power-hunting, prestige-seeking, unscrupulous, and heartless—a grievous fall indeed.

Each spiritually awakened human being who attempts transcendence of ego-consciousness encounters difficulties.[2] I-ness has become built into the human personality. This has been necessary for the unfoldment of Egoic potentialities and the development of inherent capacities.[3] I-consciousness has

2. Transcendence of ego-consciousness. The small *e* denotes personal, egotistic awareness.
3. Egoic. The capital *E* denotes purely spiritual awareness as of the reincarnating Self or Ego.

been essential in mastering the resistances of physical substance, the illusions of emotion, and the intense egoism of the more formal mind. Now, however, the procedure begins quite naturally to be reversed. This includes a change from formerly necessary self-seeking to increasingly complete self-giving. Self-concern must, in consequence, increasingly give place to concern for others. This applies, of course, to all others and not only those for whom one is more especially responsible. The ideal is ever-deepening mystical realization that one is less an individual with personal objectives and more a blend of the Will, Life, and Thought of which the universe is a manifestation and expression.

Attainment involves steady and conscientious working away at the destruction and transcendence of the separate individuality with aims and desires which apply to oneself alone. The embryo-Adept must peck his way out of this shell of separateness to emerge, not only with superhuman powers and faculties, but with ever-deepening experience attained by contemplation of his true spiritual identity. He knows himself at last to be as only a segment within THAT which is forever whole.[4]

Self-surrender is the fruit of at least two additional developments. One of these is the effect upon the mind, abstract and concrete, of influences from supraintellectual levels of being. These include intuitive insight or wisdom and completely directive will or spiritual empowerment. When these two parts of the make-up of man have become unfolded to a sufficient degree, then self-surrender takes place quite naturally and therefore effortlessly. Indeed, the consequent attitude toward life is no longer one of choice, since then no other mode of living can be followed. The other influence may be described as acquired knowledge that the very idea of self-separate existence had been and is completely untrue. Strange though this may read at first, even the concept of individuality or named identity is itself erroneous. When once this truth shines out like the light of the fully risen sun from within the depths of human nature, then self-separateness is surrendered, not only as an idea but as a motive for every major activity.

For those who, moved from within, choose the life of the cell or ashram, shutting themselves off increasingly from the ac-

4. THAT, TAT (Sk.), the Supreme Spirit.

tivities and affairs of daily life, normal objective living may continue. Because of their continued obedience to custom and necessity, such selfless ones would not appear to be much changed. Actually, however, an immense change has occurred which becomes apparent when individuals thus moved participate in unselfish service for others. They are likely to be recognized as truly inspired people, geniuses indeed, authors both in poetry and prose, planners and leaders, healers, helpers, and teachers, whether public or personal. In these ways they may reach heights of achievement far beyond the normal. In a word, they are truly inspired in work designed to increase the welfare of fellow human beings or animals. Such a person becomes the embodiment of compassionate love for all that lives and especially for all that suffers. To guide, to heal, and to help become consuming interests, and increasingly the daily life is filled with plans and action for the amelioration of the lot of living creatures.

In this, karma may play a compelling role; for the expression of the ideal and the expansion of the range of helpful influence may be limited. The value of service does not necessarily depend upon what is outwardly apparent. The usual more worldly judgments in such matters apply less and less as advancement increases. For example, Ananda-like devotion to another, in order to free the latter to assist multitudes, may be quite admirable.[5] Impersonal evaluation becomes increasingly essential as progress is made.

Success and failure, advancement and decline and, of course, really brilliant attainments on the upward way, thus have their influence upon every other member of the human family. Therefore, motives of self-gain must be discarded and metaphorically die as an ideal development, a beautification of the personal soul and bodily life. This mystical death of the lower self has to occur primarily for the sake of all mankind, and even for the sake of all that lives.

The procedure continues. Increasing numbers of immortal, spiritual souls succeed in bringing about a truly spiritual attitude of mind in their mortal personalities. This achievement leads through discontent, ardent aspiration that may not be denied, to total self-dedication to success in attaining to "the measure of the stature of the fullness of Christ," adepthood[6].

---

5. Ananda—A disciple of the Lord Gautama Buddha who performed personal services out of loving devotion to his Master.
6. Eph. 4:13.

GUIDANCE FOR ASPIRANTS CONCERNING THE SEVEN RAYS

1ST RAY

OUTSTANDING QUALITY

Kingliness.
The fire of the spiritual will.
Indomitable and decisive will power, tendng to dominate the whole life.
Heroic fortitude.

ERRORS TO BE AVOIDED

Disregard of — and overriding — the natural tendencies of others; subordination of others, particularly colleagues, and dislike amounting even to hatred of those who successfully resist.

NATURAL MODE OF SELF-EXPRESSION

Will power based upon conviction tirelessly exerted.
Rulership in every activity which is embarked upon.
This will-fire expressed through mind, emotion, and body in degree and method according to evolutionary stature.
The will to achieve indomitable rule.
Irresistible determination to carry out decisions despite all resistances.
Decisive and forceful action with an eye to the goal.

SAFEGUARDS

The attainment of deepening realization of oneness. Deeply felt respect for all deemed worthy of it. The absence of all conduct leading to constraint of others and sincere concern that all colleagues be happy in the organized activity. This happiness depends upon their freedom of action within the group-pattern. The regular and wise practice of an appropriate form of yoga.

2ND RAY

OUTSTANDING QUALITY

Wisdom arising from intuitive perception of the Divine Plan. Affection and affectionateness. Sharing in the lives of others. Helpfulness, even to sacrifice of one's own interest and wishes.

ERRORS TO BE AVOIDED

Exclusive interest in and attachment to one cause, group or person The involvement of the passions and a consuming and self-blinding desire for personal fulfillment.

NATURAL MODE OF SELF-EXPRESSION

Compassion, love, and tenderness expressed physically in service, emotionally in heart-felt feelings, mentally as deep concern for the sufferings of others, and spiritually in selfsacrificing ministrations.

SAFEGUARDS

Selflessness, mental stability, and balance, transmutation of desire. Accepted selfdiscipline and self-subordination. Exclusive interest — leading to absorption-in the fulfillment of nature's evolutionary processes. The regular and wise practice of an appropriate form of yoga.

OUTSTANDING QUALITY

Increasing ability to comprehend under-lying principles and to consider nature's laws and procedures constructively from every possible point of view. Impartiality.

NATURAL MODE OF SELF-EXPRESSION

Administration. Directorship. Logic and reason as the ultimate court of appeal. Just and fairminded solution of every problem unswayed by self-interest or personal desire.

ERRORS TO BE AVOIDED

Inhumaneness. Disinterestedness in human affairs and an unfeeling deliverance of judgments. Unavailability, withdrawal from problems which are either too demanding personally or too difficult to solve without extreme effort.

SAFEGUARDS

Balanced approaches to all decisions — human needs on the one hand and impersonal laws on the other. Personal study and self-training to be as inclusive and extensive as possible. The so called "Doctrine of the Eye" — the intellectual approach — to be supplemented by "The Doctrine of the Heart" at all levels from *Atma* to physical. Over-accentuation of one or more aspect of a question because of either external events or personal interests, to be guarded against and ultimately eliminated. *Never* conveying a decision or an order with accentuated personal disinterest or excess of detachment, which could cause undue pain from an impression of coldness. Warm heartedness throughout and after its deliverance of a judgment however unwelcome it may be to a recipient. The regular and wise practice of an appropriate form of yoga.

4TH
RAY

OUTSTANDING QUALITY

Ability to be inspired, moved or influenced — and to "perform" — from the two levels of the eternal and fundamental on the one hand and the time-ruled and changing worlds on the other. Experience of, and insistent demand for, harmony between these two — the personal and the impersonal. Desire for a harmonized coordination between the inner and outer and between oneself and others and surroundings at the levels of thought, feeling, and physical objectivity. In a phrase, beauty and beautification.

NATURAL MODE OF SELF-EXPRESSION

Method changes as the Monad-Ego unfolds its inherent powers. The relatively unevolved fourth ray person may function through the emotions and their physical experience and expression, both responding to and employing charm and allurement, and putting their minds almost to sleep in the processes. Later in their evolution, the mind skillfully employs those same procedures to other ends. Physically they respond to, depend upon even demand beauty as they see it. When eventually occultism and spirituality take an increasingly dominant place in thought and life, the fundamental cosmic principle of harmony assumes the position of Divinity or THAT which is most worshipped.

ERRORS TO BE AVOIDED

Surrender to the selfish gratification of the more personal qualities of the ray, especially to self-satisfaction and sheer pleasure. The degrading of special faculties for personal and sensual satisfaction. Neglect of mental selfdevelopment or mental idleness. Surrender to the senses. Pride in one's capacities and work for one's own gratification instead of for the presentation of the divine principle of beauty. Exhibitionism.

SAFEGUARDS

Increase lofty and selfless idealism in both the practice of an art and the living of one's life. The purification of all motives until selflessness predominates. Never exercise charm for the purposes of allurement, whether mental, emotional, physical or a combination of these. Disciplined avoidance of self-display. Purity throughout one's personal nature, so that the Divine as beauty may be granted a clean, blank "canvas" for its manifestation at one's hands. The habit of watchfulness and self-guarding against the aforementioned errors. The regular and wise practice of an appropriate form of *yoga*.

5TH
RAY

OUTSTANDING
QUALITY

An almost passionate aspiration to discover the truth, facts, and their exact interoperative relationships. This characteristic itself undergoes evolutionary development and improvement from sheer curiosity, its more primitive base, through "wanting to find out", to determine the truth for truth's sake alone. Indeed, truth, — concrete and abstract — becomes sought after and worshipped almost as if it were Deity itself, as it is for advanced fifty ray people.

NATURAL MODE OF
SELF-EXPRESSION

To search below the surface in order to discover the concealed underlying verity beneath the *maya* (illusion) of appearances. This culminates in a determination, and consequent action, to discover that ultimate Truth from which all existence at all levels arises and by which it is expressed cyclically. This begins with an instinctive, and later fully conscious, dissatisfaction with ignorance and develops into an insistent urge which cannot be denied — namely, to find the ultimate truth. Wise choice of methods, diplomatic skill, and tactical cleverness are natural to those in whom both third and fifth ray attributes are accentuated, though methods vary according to marked subrays in various incarnations.

ERRORS TO BE
AVOIDED

Dishonesty in method and practice of research and the presentation of its fruits, or in common phraseology, "trickiness". The truth may be cleverly concealed behind overwhelming verbosity or misleading phraseology while cloked in a mask of apparent frankness and fairmindedness. This is the trap which every fifth ray aspirant must carefully avoid. They must also guard against deceit in themselves and in others in conduct as well as verbally. Failing these, he or she may develop into a habitual deceiver, and in consequence, enter upon the darkened pathway.

SAFEGUARDS

Simply put, the ancient adage, "honesty is the best policy", applies especially to all those on the fifth ray who are treading the path of swift unfoldment and the byways leading to the path. They may, by unfailing practice of precision in the reception and transmission of ideas, attain their goal. Those whose parents and teachers obey and transmit the ideal of honesty in all matters, great or small, are fortunate. Elders thus have a grave responsibility, not only for their own sake, but in particular as examples to others who associate with them in whatever relationship.

6TH RAY

OUTSTANDING QUALITY

Complete dedication to a cause is a characteristic of the sixth ray. Totally selfless dedication to the fulfillment of one's own spiritual ideal and to its physical expression in service, even to the point of martyrdom. Trustworthiness and complete loyalty applied to both idealism and the association or group as well as fiery enthusiasm or burning ardor when once an ideal has been inwardly realized and accepted are also sixth ray qualities. This state might be described as one in which "nothing else matters"; the single-mindedness when nothing else and nothing less will satisfy the aspirant in pursuit of the ideal of conscious self-identification The Supreme Lord. This is no mere philosophic abstraction, but a Reality to the sixth ray person.

NATURAL MODE OF SELF-EXPRESSION

Inwardly, complete and almost overwhelmingly heartfelt devotion and its appropriate expression in mental, emotional, and physical activity, the keynote of which is Service. Instant response to urgent demands, particularly for the special kind of service to which the devotee feels drawn. In this last, more especially, the heart tends to lead the head.

ERRORS TO BE AVOIDED

A habit of being unthoughtful or vaguely focussed must be eliminated. Enthusiasm, though quite natural, may be misdirected and illfounded. Excessive haste and failure to fully consider proposals and all its implications and possible effects, as well as failure to consider alternate proposals for service and effective methods before going into action. An immediate call into action. An immediate response to a call for service may be a virtue, it also has its hazards if done too precipitously. Emotionally derived, personally desired methods should be carefully weighed even if they later prove to be the best choices. Avoid undue personalization of one's work or subdue it to the more impersonal outlook of the true devotee.

SAFEGUARDS

An effective, practicable, blending of fiery will, careful thought, and loving heart will always be the greatest safeguard against errors — particularly that of impetuosity. All impulses should ideally be carefully subjected to judgment by the intellect. They should not allow depression to follow an apparent failure, nor heartbreak to result from personal loss or incident of disloyalty. Should these dull the enthusiasm or dedication, the sixth ray person may suffer delay in their active expression in service. Meditation on and application to all activity of wise discrimination are amongst the best safeguards against error by all devotees. Careful choice of the best time, place and method is, indeed, an urgent necessity. Zeal is most valuable, but it should not override reason. The regular and wise practice of an appropriate form of yoga.

7TH
RAY

OUTSTANDING QUALITY

Will-power, intellectual concepts, idealism and appropriate action are the hallmarks of the seventh ray man. The spiritually awakened seventh ray man or woman is a person of action with driving enthusiasm and they eventually acquire an overmastering intensity of concentrated will-thought. In the awakened, this can lead to error. Awakened in the occult sense, it lifts individuals far above the trammels of personal interests, even planetary concerns; for seventh ray man is treading a pathway which leads to solar and cosmic levels and degrees of activity. These solar energies and intelligences increasingly become his sources and collaborators. Exalted, he knows the cosmos as a single whole. Rather than specialize in one field or method, he or she synthezes — coordinates into a whole — all that is being handled and cared for, always to the end of a balanced harmonization.

NATURAL MODE OF SELF-EXPRESSION

Human beings in whom the seventh ray attributes predominate are instinctively, naturally moved toward orderliness in everything they do. In consequence, they are ritualistic by nature. Life and the process of living become for them a stately, dignified, and ordered ceremonial. Occultly and spiritually awakened or called upon to invoke, employ and radiate spiritualizing energies, they find progressively arranged ceremonials are the most acceptable and effective ways of performing the tasks and fulfilling such duties. They are ceremonialists by nature.

ERRORS TO BE AVOIDED

Until a certain evolutionary stature has been reached, the outer form and the details of chosen rituals can mentally imprison the ritualist. Procedure then dominates objectives. Means can become ends in themselves instead of instruments whereby purposes are fulfilled. Mechanization can threaten the effectiveness of the worker, particularly in fields of occult science. In due course, ultimate objectives dominate the mind, and ritual performances receive only sufficient attention to ensure their complete effectiveness. Office and the prestige resulting from its attainment endanger both the sincerity and the effectiveness. Against this error, all ceremonies — and therefore all seventh ray operators — must be on guard.

SAFEGUARDS

Guarding against such errors is best attained by the regular practice of yoga — notably a combination of *Mantra* and *Raja* — and by constant reminding the self that effectiveness in occult procedures *depends almost entirely upon selflessness.* Even the slightest tinge of self inevitably reduces the effectiveness as well as the amount of spiritual energy or force which can be generated or evoked during ceremonial and so its effectiveness in the work to be done. Personal attainment and pride in it inevitably distorst concepts concerning purposes for such activity and so gravely reduces effectiveness. The Law ordains that he or she who consistently puts self before service is condemned to ineffectiveness. Exercise watchfulness, complete humility, dispassion and disinterestedness as far as oneself is concerned, and a total absorption in the work itself — these are the most effective safeguards against degradation of both the performers and the rituals they perform.

12

Selfishness Beyond Death

THE IDEA HELD in certain religious Sects that dramatic changes and purifications occur to the soul after passage through the gateway of death needs to be received with marked reserve, even with doubt. Indeed, the duly qualified clairvoyant observer who, with direct vision, studies the experiences into which a person enters on awakening in the superphysical worlds after physical death, testifies that no actual change of character is seen to occur. The deceased is, in general, found to be quite unchanged in all the essentials of his or her personal nature displayed during physical life. Most certainly, it is averred, human beings do not change into angels immediately after bodily death. On the contrary, they remain in most respects much as they were before that event.[1]

This being the case, those who have surrendered during life to mental, emotional, and physical errors for personal gain, hitherto described, find themselves mentally and morally imprisoned behind the walls and bars of habitual outlook, tendencies, and conduct. Moreover, those who are enclosed within self-built prisons formed of self-centeredness and selfishness prove to be almost unreachable by those who would offer aid and suggest means of escape. Thus, bereft of or unresponsive to aid from without, and selfishly concerned with personal gain at all costs, they tend mentally to sink deeper and deeper into the darkened enclosure which they have so consistently built for themselves.

When *self* becomes the name of the deity which they worship, they become increasingly unresponsive to, and so cut off

1. See *Through the Gateway of Death,* Geoffrey Hodson.

from, divine assistance, whether from without or within themselves. The results of all their self-inspired deeds are inescapable. The mental attitude, the motivation of self-gain at no matter what cost to principles or persons, remains as the sole impulse to which they had become slaves and still remain in slavery. For such people after physical death, spiritual impulses find greater and greater resistance, until at last they are no longer experienced to any degree. In terms of vibrating forces, spiritualizing energies no longer reach them. This is the condition which in Eastern occultism is referred to as *avitchi*, meaning waveless.[2]

A reference is here made to the further teaching of occult science that the substance of a universe becomes arranged in successive degrees of density. The hardness of the physical mineral represents the extreme wherein the rays of the sun do not easily penetrate. Such a condition does not actually exist at the superphysical levels of consciousness and being into which the soul of man enters after physical death. There exists, nevertheless, a state corresponding to mineral consciousness and a substance into which the rays of the spiritual sunlight and life cannot enter—one might almost say a location—in which these fallen ones are then obliged to reside.

Such beings are *never* entirely beyond the reach of spiritualizing aid. Those close to adeptship are called upon to bring help to such dwellers in darkness or "souls in prison."[3] Many factors govern the possibility and the amount of response to proffered help of which such a deceased person is capable. One factor is Law, the operation of nature's inevadable—but not unmodifiable—law of cause and effect. Another influence consists of the extent to which the surrender to sheer selfishness had progressed before death. For example, actions of a kindly and even unselfish nature would contribute to the possibility of response to aid. If, furthermore, there had been periods during physical life in which the voice of conscience had caused the person to seek the aid of religion and prayer, then the law of cause and effect could doubtless be modified on his behalf. His capacities for responsiveness would certainly have become built into the character and so also the ability to answer favorably to spiritual aid.

2. *Avitchi* (Sk.) "Waveless," as described in the text, meaning unresponsive to spiritual vibrations.
3. 1 Peter 3:18-19.

Therefore, when a sainted and powerfully illumined initiate at very great cost of suffering enters the world of the utterly fallen ones in their afterdeath state, there will be some who are not only capable of response, but, perhaps in their despair or with gratitude, will actually grasp the hand outstretched to save them. Great power and great love are needed for success in this rescue operation, and rescuers have achieved these qualities. Therefore, rescued ones do from time to time arise from the utterly darkened world into realms illumined by the sunlight of truth and selflessness.

Unless they have utterly, completely and deliberately cut themselves off from their divine Source, every human being is a manifestation of a spiritual Monad. Since rescue operations are successfully carried out, there cannot exist among humanity a condition that is erroneously referred to as "an eternally lost soul." However, in a small number of cases, descent into the deepest degrees of selfishness, and the deliberate performance of self-motivated actions without regard for the sufferings inflicted upon others, mysteriously cuts the individual off from the monadic Source. A slow and very painful process of disintegration of the erstwhile personality then occurs. In such rare cases, the word *failure* becomes written over the evolutionary history since individualization as a self-conscious entity occurred.[4] What may be described as a new beginning must then be made. The level at which a fresh start must be made is dependent upon the degree of self-degradation by selfishness which had led to the downfall.

These ideas—drawn from the esoteric wisdom and the indelible records—are in no sense offered in order to cause distress. They are presented in order to accentuate the warnings against selfishness—mankind's true and only "curse," self-invoked as it is—and to strengthen the appeal for increasing selflessness. The aspirant must be ever on guard against this demon of self-interest which may remain from former modes of living and grow into a veritable "devil" of destructiveness. I, as author of this book, would fail grievously should I not thus draw attention to and give warning against the one danger that threatens every awakening and newly awakened human being.

4. Individualization: A change experienced by the Monad (Man's innermost Spirit-Self) on passing from incarnation in the animal kingdom (group soul) into the human. See *A Study in Consciousness*, A. Besant, and *Lecture Notes of the School of the Wisdom*, Vol. 1, Geoffrey Hodson.

If this proffered guidance should seem to involve an undue urgency, it is because the effects of deliberate denials of the ideals unfailingly and universally stressed by the Teachers who visit mankind, follow the individual into his or her existence after bodily death. In very truth, after-death conditions are formulated and imposed by one's conduct during the period of physical life.

13

Truth, Knowledge, and Intuition

THE ACCENTUATION of selfless love, beautifully called "The Doctrine of the Heart," must be balanced by an understanding of the underlying laws of nature upon which the objective universe is founded and by which it is maintained. Those who at any stage of their lives discover this Divine Wisdom are fortunate. Still more fortunate are those who find and intuitively accept that secret knowledge which leads directly to God-consciousness. A new world of inquiry, thought, and study then opens before such awakening ones. They experience an almost passionate longing for still deeper wisdom and the opportunity to study and apply it to the processes of living.

In general, the safest touchstone consists of that wisdom of the ages known in the West as Theosophy and in the East as both *Brahmavidya* and *Guptavidya*.[1] Serious-minded and selflessly motivated students who aspire to become illumined by knowledge which is reasonably correct are advised to study these sources. In addition, they may well be used as tests for growing comprehension.

The truth discovered and delivered to mankind by the sages is at least twofold, particularly concerning its relatively public availability. The two Sanskrit words referred to above—*Brahmavidya* and *Guptavidya*—indicate that certain of the fruits of adeptic research are reserved from public exposition, while others are offered more freely to all fortunate enough to discover and to study them. In Sanskrit the latter are

---

1. *Brahmavidya* (Sk.) Knowledge about the Supreme Deity. *Guptavidya* (Sk.) Esoteric knowledge.

called *Brahmavidya*—the Wisdom of Brahma, the Supreme Deity. When, however, the inmost depths of such knowledge are referred to, they are named *Guptavidya*—the Secret Wisdom. While *Brahmavidya* is reasonably intelligible and can prove to be a great source of enlightenment, *Guptavidya* may seem very mysterious, and those who propound it give the impression of strange reserve. In English these two methods of delivering truth may be named *exoteric* and *esoteric,* or revealed and secret, respectively.

Strangely, the revealed and the hidden Wisdom in certain ways appear to be in conflict and even to contradict each other. This is not true, of course, as far as ultimate knowledge is concerned, but only in methods of presentation. Just as information is gradually put before scholars at preparatory and normal schools, precollege and university institutions, so the esoteric wisdom is made available in graduated forms. The limitation of knowledge characteristic of the early years may cause it to *appear* to contradict that which is revealed later on. This is also true in the study of what might be referred to as the Arcana.[2] As when viewing natural scenery, the aspects appear different according to the points of view from which observations are made. The total scenery, however, in itself remains unchanged.

The necessity for entering the "child-state" during the search for wisdom may be regarded as an example of apparent, but never real, contradiction between the hidden and revealed Wisdom.[3] A child cannot be expected to grasp advanced mathematics, science, or philosophy. Why then the injunction? A state of mind rather than bodily age is obviously being referred to. The child-mind has not as yet become either naturally or self-protectively overegoistic; moreover, it is simple, and this absence of complication contributes to successful education in the earlier years. This child-state has its direct applications to the successful reception of esoteric ideas by an adult. The development of either a protective or even bigoted mental state, or a sense of self-importance, creates an almost impassable barrier to the entry of esoteric wisdom into the mind and into the region within it where the faculty of comprehension abides. This is because the ideas are completely impersonal in their very nature and totally universal in their

2. Arcana, Mysteries.
3. Matt. 18:3-4.

outworkings or expressions. No one can possibly possess them and claim them as one's own. They belong to everybody, to all life and all intelligence, extending as they do from the divine point or Source outward to the cosmos as a whole. A physical illustration might be drawn from the universal law of gravity which affects all objects and cannot be possessed by any one of them.

For example, the instruction from the Mystery Tradition is difficult if not impossible to understand if a person's knowledge of human existence is limited to the attributes of the physical body which is born and most certainly will die. To speak of eternal life, the undying continuance of existence, to a person whose only view of mankind is physical, would evoke a protesting, demanding, and even arrogant denial. This response is quite natural and even desirable from one whose point of view is solely physical, but if obstinately adhered to, it would impose a serious barrier to the reception of the truth.

A child, on the other hand, might still retain such respect for his or her elders as to be quite open to receive without resistance information that for the time is beyond childish powers of direct comprehension. In this sense only, and not as an encouragement to blind or slavish acceptance of orthodoxy, the child-state is essential to the acceptance and eventual comprehension of esoteric wisdom. The key to success in this endeavor consists of complete selflessness; for the moment a thought of self at any level of human consciousness and activity enters the field of the mind, a barrier is interposed between that mind—shadowed as it has become—and truth itself.

The example chosen may perchance prove useful if still further applied to the receipt of sacred knowledge by a neophyte. Under occult guidance and training the inner eye is gradually opened and the affirmation of immortality becomes an observable fact. Moreover, extended research into areas such as life after physical death becomes possible. That first moment of intuitive receptiveness—not argument—is essential in acquiring occult knowledge, and it is this spontaneous responsiveness which is included in the child-state. Such a condition applies mainly to the commencement of occult training.

Only those who can provide the evolutionary mental and psychological conditions that render them suitable for the receipt of the *Guptavidya,* the Secret Wisdom, can receive such teachings. These are the chosen ones from the point of view of the Master who accepts disciples; for he is able to discern infallibly whether or not such qualifications exist in the potential trainee. This is referred to and illustrated by Jesus who, immediately on seeing certain of his disciples, called upon them to "follow me."[4] The child-state is exemplified in the response of those who were fishermen, for example, for "straightway they left their nets, and followed him."[5] On the other hand, the rich young man lacked a certain openness, simplicity, dispassion and non-egoism. He could not comply with the Master's description of the essential conditions, because of personal possessiveness indicated by his reason for refusal, namely "for he had great possessions."[6]

Scriptural narratives describe events occurring in the course of daily life and to people engaged in the business of fishing and supervision. However, it is more usual for the call to be heard and the teaching to be received in the seclusion of a temple of the Mysteries, where the necessary isolation is provided.

Accounts of what on the surface appear to be quite ordinary, if not casual, examples of human intercourse, to the illumined mind can convey profound truths. These concern the unfoldment of intuitive and spiritual powers and capacities under the guidance of an adept Teacher. That essential capacity in a human being which makes the right response possible, may be described as "intuitive instinctiveness" that operates without the intervention of reasoning, especially of argument or resistance. A child's immediate and joyous acceptance of pleasure-giving, tasteful food is instinctual and not based upon the reasoning which develops later in life. Similarly, instant response to the call and readiness for the immense privilege of discipleship require the child state when that great privilege is accepted. The opened Portal leading into the outer court of a temple of the Mysteries is intuitively and instinctively sought by such an aspirant, even though a complete understanding of the interior experience has not yet been attained.

Attention may here again be drawn to the necessity for self-purification in the widest meaning of that word. Motives, psychological states, and physical ways of life must all be cleansed of undue self-interest. Mental and emotional im-

4. Matt. 4:19.
5. Mark 1:18.
6. Matt. 19:16-23.

purities and physical interests and activities that, tested against the new ideal, are to be regarded as unacceptable, will naturally be renounced. It is not difficult to perceive the reasons for self-imposition of this age-old rule if spiritual wisdom is to be received and spiritual vision to be successfully developed. Just as a completely clear glass is necessary for clarity and accuracy in looking through the glass both from within and from without, so the mental "panes of glass" must be perfectly clean and clear. As cleanliness is needed still more in optical research, similarly, the windows and telescopes of the mind must be absolutely clean and clear if acquired knowledge, external and interior, is to be true and meticulously accurate. As a soiled instrument may deliver false information, so also soiled psychological equipment for the attainment of knowledge may result in errors and inexactitudes which may prove to be very dangerous indeed.

Mistakes at these early stages of the most important undertaking upon which man embarks, must always be most carefully guarded against. This is stressed, not only because it is true in the general search for knowledge, but also because false concepts at the very beginning of the search can lead an individual astray for the whole of the remaining years of his life. Above all, the seeker is warned concerning the very natural and human tendency to regard his own temporary findings—useful as they may be—as superior to the teachings of the Wisdom of the Ages. A gradually deepening approach to and comprehension of these teachings is completely necessary if the truly great spiritual heights are to be discerned and ultimately ascended.

Thought-processes involved in such study bring one to an appreciation of the almost immeasurable importance of the power now beginning to awaken in modern man, namely direct supramental awareness of truth or, in a word, intuition. Almost immediately, one is confronted by the strange fact that the processes of the logical and translogical mind—concrete and abstract—valuable though they have been, must now be discarded as readily as once they were sought. This does not imply in the least degree that *unreason* should supplant reason, but rather that mind and supramental awareness penetrate more and more completely through the veil of innumerable illusions which formerly seemed so very real.

For example, man advancing on the pathway which leads from temporary to eternal truth, from illusion to Reality, must

71

discover the real nature of both electricity and *prana* or vital energy.[7] In the fields of science and technology discoveries have been tested and proven by their application to the production of phenomena. Whenever an electric switch is turned to the *on* position, for example—all else being correctly prepared—the current at once begins to flow. Nevertheless, the nature and source of the electrical energy itself are, as yet, entirely unknown. Truths such as this are still heavily veiled, hidden from the most penetrating, organized, and developed human mind.

Similarly, the existence of that vital principle, the absence or the presence of which distinguishes between the conditions of life and death, has not yet been determined by science. At least one other factor besides organic changes such as the heartbeat differentiates between a deceased and a living human body. True, it might be said that certain life processes become active in the deceased body to produce the phenomenon of decay. Others must, in consequence, be presumed also to be present which *prevent* decay during life. What, then, is the nature of these influences and of the principle or power which produces them in such marked differentiation? It is that mysterious factor or principle called prana or Life in Occult Science.

Despite the most remarkable discoveries and developments achieved by the human mind up to the present time, man lives and moves in a universe and a personal environment moved by laws, processes, and forces concerning which he knows little or nothing. How can man really come to know the nature, the procedures, and the manifold interrelationships of that nameless life principle so markedly active within and all about him? The science of physics with its applications of mathematics to natural processes is a guide to that which is hidden behind and within the laws and procedures of the time-imprisoned universe. But physics must lead to metaphysics; for Truth itself in complete reality is veiled behind the laws of time, space, and alternation. Until mankind and its individual representatives find and, inwardly impelled, pass through the gateway and outer court leading from intellectual learning to intuitional knowing, the guardian doors of the temple of Truth itself will ever be closed. The human mind may well shrink from what appears to transcend science, but

7. *Prana* (Sk.) Cosmic Life manifesting on all planes. The Breath of life.

that shrinking must be overcome. In this age of the awakening and development of the human intuitive faculty, direct interior experience of philosophic truths is the aim—the goal at the intellectual level—for all those who are in search of Truth itself. Discovery of one's own truth in one's own terms is possible for the truly persistent seeker for knowledge.

Truth thus envisaged, is as a Sun which never sets, a light that is never dimmed. On the contrary, it grows more potent and more brilliant as the aspirant rises from mind to intuition. This transcendence of the limitations of science—from physics to metaphysics—is the real Deacon principle by which candidates for initiation are conducted round the Masonic lodge, respresenting the temple of the Mysteries. All rites, especially secret rites, aid men or women in the deeply interior processes of awakening, developing, and using the intuitive faculty. Whether this or other practices are followed, increasingly exclusive concentration upon the primary ideal of the attainment of direct knowledge is required. The secondary purpose is the delivery of that knowledge to mankind for the welfare of humanity.

The dawning intuitive expression of the cosmic seed within the human Monad, irresistibly leads men on, first to physical and then to metaphysical heights. Many lives will be required before the brain-mind of an inquirer is sufficiently developed to be able to comprehend the teachings of the sages concerning the great mystery of human life and its evolution to perfection. Reality cannot adequately be explained in terms of conceptual thinking. Even though Truth may be approached conceptually, the discursive intellect does not readily reach reality. The formal mind is incurably concrete and objective. In consequence, the human spirit can become imprisoned in the illusory labyrinth of the mind, as is allegorically portrayed in the Greek myth of the Minotaur.

A somewhat drastic change must eventually take place, difficult to achieve and most difficult to describe. This is because spiritual experience transcends the thinking process, so that attempted descriptions become overlaid with words, which imprison abstract ideas as in a straightjacket. The human unit of consciousness is thus normally enwrapped in a cocoon, a web of perishable substances, of three-dimensional space and forms. Mind identifies itself with and is spellbound by this illusion, believing this as its own experience. On the other

73

hand, contemplation leads beyond the intellect back into the one real world which is always there in its undivided wholeness. In the higher consciousness, dimensions lose their significance; for there exists neither up nor down, far away nor near, in either place or time. All is present in fullness, so that without any movement in space whatever one may realize the very subtlest modes of manifestation of the one divine Principle, the one informing Life in all. Unity with that Life is implicit and not the result of discussion.

Spiritual awareness is barrierless, includes "neither darkness nor shadow of turning"[8] and, when consciousness is wholly centered at formless levels, it is incapable of experiencing the objective pairs of opposites, for only the positives of these pairs can be included in supramental perception. This is not a condition to be reached by reasoning alone. All too often, it defies intellectual determination. Those who have experienced it are frequently at a loss to explain it coherently or logically, and moreover, when it is explained, its content more or less undergoes mutilation. Indeed, Egoic consciousness is characterized by incommunicability; for the inner Self of man abides in pure, simple, absolute awareness, radiant with its own light, expressing itself spontaneously in a secret infinity of joy. A continuing harmonious happiness exists, mounting to serene ecstasy, indescribable bliss. Sometimes this serenity and happiness can pervade the personal nature, producing in it a similar sense of harmoniousness and pleasure, bestowing upon physical experience a sense of the beauty and even sweetness of life.

14

Realizing Unity

THE UNIVERSE ITSELF, with its indwelling Life, is an evolving
production. Matter gradually becomes more sensitive and
more responsive to Life, which in its turn becomes more potent
in matter. Thus, in the very process of cosmic development
duality is implicit, namely indwelling Life and ensheathing or
embodying matter. A third principle consists of the interlink-
ing power of mind, whereby and wherein experience is gained
throughout the whole evolutionary procedure.[1] Mind may
thus be regarded as the awareness principle throughout all
kingdoms of nature. Consciousness, particularly of that which
is external, appears to unfold very slowly, so heavily does the
sheer weight of inert matter imprison the Life principle.

A humanity which does not know by experience of this
duality—particularly in the human constitution, physical and
superphysical—and which in consequence pays little or no
attention to the relationship between life and substance except
for an occasional prayer, perhaps, fails to approach life and the
problems of life in depth, as it were. Naturally, even design-
edly, while he is awake, man is conscious of himself largely as a
bodily person. This is the great mistake from which so many
human problems and difficulties arise. Because of this un-
awareness, man does not recognize the necessity for a good
working arrangement between inner and outer self. This is
exactly the reason for so much human error, lack of knowledge, and even ill-health. The regular practice of some means
of preserving and increasing interior and external harmony is

1. *Mahat* (Sk.) Universal Mind.

essential to the avoidance of the resultant errors. Church and temple services and customary daily prayer only partly meet this necessity.

The remedy for these and so many other human ills consists largely of a regular practice of communion between the immortal and eternal spiritual being within and the mortal, transient physical vehicle or temple in which it is enshrined. In consequence, from childhood and as soon as development permits, everyone should practice some form of prayer, yoga, or *puja*.[2] The aim of this is less to obtain personal benefits from a presumed celestial Source than to evoke and receive corrective and healing energies from one's own divine nature, the God dwelling within the man of flesh.

Primitive man uses primitive means as he seeks to obtain contact with that power, the existence of which his experience of life reveals to him. While advanced man may smile—even derisively—nevertheless primeval man is exhibiting, almost in humility and awe, a tendency to seek aid from an instinctively believed-in superior power. Ceremony comes to his aid, and as man evolves, among some people ceremonies become increasingly complex, and also more beautiful and intelligently composed and performed. In consequence, their helpfulness increases—particularly for certain temperaments—as they are refined and more definitely directed toward communication with and guidance from the Divine.

One advantage of ceremonial, whether recognized or not, is that the mind is distracted from the outer phenomenal world and directed toward the interior world wherein spiritual reality is to be found. Prayers, invocations, psalms, and hymns provide vocal means of expressing devotion toward and trust in the Divine. Movements of the body and its vestments, and the employment of symbols used from the remotest times, combine to elevate consciousness from the earth to heaven where the supreme Deity is presumed to have its dwelling place.

Eventually, the need—demand indeed—for more direct communication with spiritual realms and beings, and for states of consciousness in which they may be contacted, reduces the use of ceremonial and increases personal endeavor. The seeker begins the search for God, whether as an abstract principle, a discoverable "Person" or even Three Persons. Such

2. *Puja* (Sk.) Hindu religious ceremony.

seeking may begin with a more or less simple interest but deepens to become a yearning. This assumes so great a power over the mind that the call to the highest must be responded to by the most appropriate endeavors. The word *appropriate* is of overriding significance. The most effective method is sought, both from literary sources and by means of experiments with differing physical and mental approaches.

In the East from time immemorial the practice of yoga —particularly in terms of states of consciousness rather than bodily actions and postures alone—has provided an efficient method for reaching the God within. As far as his inner life is concerned, it may truthfully be said that the great need of mankind in the present age—and always—is the intimately personal practice day by day of a method of yoga. This Sanskrit word meaning identity, union, oneness, here applies to any and all sincere and dedicated efforts to achieve self-spiritualization, whether they be Eastern or Western, ancient or modern. Every problem by which mankind is confronted may be solved by yoga and yoga alone. This book would be incomplete unless it contained guidance in the practice of yoga as both a meditative procedure and a scientific method that can be applied to every aspect of human life.

What then should be the nature of yoga practice? It consists of quiet and regular contemplation, purity of life, and conduct based upon the ideal of family relationship. The contemplation includes a carefully ordered regime of self-training. Its rules and all necessary guidance have long been available as they are today.

In the beginning a somewhat formal routine is practiced. This will vary with the individual according to his Ray, his physical circumstances, including health, and his general tendencies of mental activity.[3] By experiment a procedure is found, developed, and regularly used which is suitable and adaptable to the nature and temperament of the individual concerned. Guided by available information, each would-be yogi finds, fashions, and follows his or her own techniques.

Some people may, for example, find, or at least attempt to find, their pathway to the realization of unity with the Divine through the ever-increased perfection of their work, whether manual, cultural, or intellectual. Self-perfecting through all

3. Ray, accentuated characteristic. See *The Seven Human Temperaments,* Geoffrey Hodson.

activities will assume a dominating position in their practice of yoga—karma yoga. At first, such workers seek continual improvement largely for its own sake. Gradually, however, the realization dawns that there is but one worker, namely the Godhead at work throughout the whole Cosmos and that same Godhead incarnate as the true Self of man. Thereafter consciously, intuitively, and with total effort of will, all work is performed more and more in God's name and for God as the one supreme Worker of all. All work becomes divine activity and must therefore be carried out as effectively, beautifully, and logically as possible. The personality of the server fades, to be replaced by the spirit of the divine Architect and Artificer of the universe.

Others, by methods appropriate to themselves according to temperament, move toward the same objective of mergence with the Godhead and ultimate disappearance therein. Religion for these men and women consists of an ever-deepening realization of this fundamental fact of unity. Indeed, the religious life is for them an ever more effective application of the power which is God, to both the perfection of their own lives and the ordering of communities, great and small, according to divine rule. This unification is the true goal in the practice of yoga: divine thought, intuitive wisdom, and will are then known to be inherent within every yogi and also in the totality of creation. Identity with this is seen as implicit, the illusion of duality having virtually disappeared. The yogi or yogini consciously melts,[4] knowing himself or herself forever merged into that nameless Principle which can only be referred to as Beingness, or in Sanskrit *Sat*.[5]

Experience of this kind inevitably affects the character, the morality, and the self-control of one who makes the great discovery. As this state is consciously approached, method, system, and practice make increasingly reduced demands, become decreasingly necessary, essential as they were earlier. Strange though the statement may sound, even the goal of experienced unity with the Life principle disappears, founded erroneously as it was upon the idea of duality, the blending of two supposedly separate beings or states of consciousness and existence. This is replaced by the transcendental awareness that only One exists and that the yogi is that One. This is

4. Yogini—female yogi.
5. *Sat* (Sk.) Being; Existence; the most abstract expression for the Godhead.

samadhi or Nirvana.[6] When once it is attained, method, system, practice as distinct efforts are no longer needed; for the goal has been achieved. This is not the realized unification of *two* which have been separate or diverse, but identity with that which is the *One* alone.

As mankind quite naturally travels the evolutionary pathway, this state of realized oneness will become more easily attained. Not only do the capacities of human consciousness to understand and experience oneness increase, but also the matter or substance of the brain itself offers decreasing resistance. The attribute or guna of inertia,[7] which has played a large part in imprisoning consciousness in the jail of separateness, begins to lose its imprisoning power. Matter itself has been the real jailer and its imprisoning functions will continue to be difficult to overcome for a time. This is why the emphasis has so consistently been placed on regular continuity, day by day and even hour by hour, of the practice of yoga, whether as prayer or as contemplation of oneness with the Divine. The task before the yogi is to override, transcend, the limitations imposed upon consciousness by matter—as far as concrete thought, experienced and expressed emotions and physical objects are concerned. Very gradually, in most if not in all cases, the student will be taught how to establish the center of self-awareness in progressively subtler vehicles so that he or she learns at will to focus attention in any one of these. The means, of course, consists of thought processes. One imagines oneself in a positive, constructive manner as being aware, briefly, but with realism, in the body and world of feelings. Then one thinks of oneself in the realm of the mentality of the normal thinking processes. This is designed to elevate the range of vibratory, and so conscious, responsiveness of the brain cells and therefore of the brain-mind. When successful, this brings the student to the threshold of his spiritual being and consciousness.

This is a dual process. On the one hand, it consists of the gradual unfoldment from latency to full potency of man's threefold spiritual attributes. On the other hand, his progress consists of the evolution of his four material vehicles to a

6. *Samadhi* (Sk.), the yogic state in which the ascetic loses the consciousness of every individuality, including his own. Nirvana (Sk.), the final state of human evolution, where the consciousness is expanded to embrace the cosmos. See Glossary.

7. *Guna* (Sk.), attribute of matter. See Glossary.

condition in which they perfectly make manifest his threefold spiritual powers. Inner unfoldment is accompanied by the outer development of the bodies until they become a more perfect temple and expression of the inner God.

Yoga might thus be described in terms of one of its main objectives, as a means of ever more intimate intercommunication between brain and spiritual intelligence, between moral man and the true immortal Self. The true yogi is thus in no sense a dreamer, nor is he or she a person who spends *only* so much time day-by-day in certain physical postures and in the performance of certain mental and spiritual activities. Though these may continue to have their place in daily life, the time allotted for them grows less and less as the yogi comes naturally to live in fully conscious experience of the divine, eternal individuality, the *true* Self. Sages have ever taught that yoga, thus regarded, is less a withdrawal into meditation for a certain time each day—important though that is—than a way of life, a recognition of, and communion with the Divine which encompasses the whole of life.

Realization of unity may be achieved in several ways. The yogi may learn to lift the level of used and operative consciousness above the limitations of concrete thinking, up to the region of abstract and relatively form-free states of being and intelligence. Or he may acquire the faculty of knowing, feeling, and sensing the presence of the ever-fluidic, form-free, all-pervading Life-principle, both within and outside of all forms. Or he may combine both of these until at last the so-called "flight of the soul" from the imprisonment of matter and form becomes possible, and is in fact achieved. This leads to a deepening realization of his intimate spiritual relationship with all his fellowmen. When this is sufficiently developed and becomes the ruling power and principle in motive and action, then awareness of and responsiveness to beings and conditions even beyond the planet may begin to be acquired.

Though there are many yogic practices, a few are sufficient to enable the self-trained yogi to enter and eventually to live within yogic illumination as a perpetual state. The essentials are the chanting of a single effective mantram, the skillful establishment of the center of thought and knowledge in the threefold spiritual Self within, and bodily stillness. The mind, too, must be rendered reasonably still, mental activities concerned with time, space, and forms reduced to a minimum.

The rush of intellectual concepts that might enter the vacuum eventually must cease. In the almost wondrous silence which seems of itself to occupy the mental field, stillness becomes the condition of the quietened mind and gradually pervades the entire consciousness. Gradually, effortlessly, conceptual thinking gives place to what may only be described as time-free, form-free, place-free realization of the inmost nature of those things which have been excluded from the mind. Inmost aptly describes both these illuminations and their source. In what is almost—but not entirely—emptiness, the supramental and hitherto totally incomprehensible basis for all that exists enters awareness. At first, this is not understandable, if only because it stretches the mind beyond human understanding and normal ability even to consider such. It brings realization that the true foundation of the universe is a principle or THATNESS which is without limitations such as geographical designation, defined edges or limitations, enclosure of any kind, and especially even of a mental ideal of limitation. The One Life is THAT which is everywhere without limit, ever-existing without beginning or end, and—though words inevitably fail—ever-inclusive, implying that there is nowhere and no time at which it does not exist.[8] The attempt—quite natural—to bestow upon it attributes of any kind fails completely as long as the realizing center of consciousness is maintained and preserved in the utmost, formless state. For the fundamental Principle is neither wavelike nor still, unacceptable though such a contradiction is to the mind. It is neither colorless nor colored, neither rhythmic nor motionless, not only here and now, but also everywhere and always. These utterly and admittedly incomprehensible opposite attributes that normally would destroy any product of conceptual thought are nevertheless revealed from the depths of purely spiritual awareness. The best name for the everywhere indwelling Principle is *THAT*.

The above statements may well and even permissibly be dismissed as purest nonsense; for they are nonsense to a mind functioning only in sensory terms. However, in a contemplative state the ever unseen interior of the tip of the cornucopia can be realized.[9] The symbology is suggestive; for the forever

8. See *A Yoga of Light,* Geoffrey Hodson.
9. Cornucopia—Latin *Cornu copeae*—classical symbol of plenty, consisting of goat's or bull's horn overflowing with flowers and fruits, possessed by the nymph Amalthea of Greek mythology.

unknowable underlying Principle is nevertheless the Source from which all nature and all natural products or gifts are emanated into the objective worlds. Having arrived there, they become available in prodigal abundance, an unlimited and time-free supply of all that man can ever need. The vast and largely incomprehensible procedure under which life in mineral becomes life in plant, animal, man, and thereafter Adept also emanates from that invisible and unknowable Source. Its objective beginning could perhaps also be likened to the tip of the cornucopia.

15

Discipleship

WHEN THE MORE DEEPLY hidden aspects of man's nature begin to awaken from occult sleep, and the interior and the external life of the person begins to be affected thereby, then, as earlier stated, an adeptic representative of the Greater Mysteries becomes aware of the fact. Guidance reaches the awakening individual, and as he responds to it, a closer and more conscious relationship between himself and the Teacher becomes established. The neophyte now becomes the disciple of an adept Master. This is a most striking and important development, particularly because of the possibilities open for hastened progress. To the extent that the disciple can endure and benefit from forcing the pace—very much the Master's responsibility—he begins to overstep the normal limits and stages of human evolution toward the state of Adeptship.[1] This experience is associated with the more occult evolution of man and especially of the reincarnating Self which with its personal vehicles later becomes an initiate and eventually an Adept.

The experience of becoming the recipient of spiritual counsel—though appearing on occasion to have been almost accidental—is very carefully planned by the adept Teacher. Worthiness, as already stated, is the first consideration, and the proposed recipient's mode of life, general motives for living, and degree of spiritual awakening, are also carefully considered. The intelligence or reasonableness of the individual

1. See *The Pathway to Perfection*, Geoffrey Hodson.

must in its turn be evaluated, if only to discover the extent to which spiritual intervention is sensibly received.

While a human parent cares for the physical and intellectual progress of a son or daughter, the adept "parent" leaves physical welfare to the disciple and concentrates upon mental and spiritual unfoldment. *Unfoldment* truly describes the relationship; for the Master's influence is applied not only from without, but far more, from within. While wise and loving parents guide and instruct their offspring by example and verbal instruction, the Master by his very presence evokes hitherto dormant spiritual capacities. These include an iron will, a direct intuitive perception, and a continually expanding knowledge, grasp, and application to motives of the fundamental principles of divine manifestation, for despite apparent diversities at all levels the underlying laws and procedures are ever the same.

Thus inspired (rather than instructed), the growth of the disciple, may be rapid. The Master watches over him lest the very newness of the spiritual, intuitive, and intellectual experiences lead to mistakes in their applications to daily living. This possibility is very real and the history of the path from its beginning on earth reveals both failures and successes.

In addition to the purely human or personal relationships between disciple and Master with their highly beneficial effects (such as are described concerning the Christ and the Buddha) there begins and is extended, the reception of guidance and teaching. These concern the deeper aspects of human nature and their correspondences with substances and high intelligences existing in the regions of extraplanetary space. Receipt of the secret wisdom—usually by a pledged disciple from his Master—not only bestows a supernormal potency upon the mind and outer personality of the recipient, but is also power-bestowing in itself.[2] This could perhaps be somewhat likened to presumed stimulation and increase of a person's brain-power by the application to it of a current of electricity on the one hand, and the limitless potentialities existing in the current itself and its sources, on the other.

Because of both the greatly heightened sensitivity which

2. Some of these beneficial effects were: the hastening of human evolution toward perfection; spiritual guidance; bestowal of heightened capacity to teach, heal, exorcise evil spirits; write inspiring accounts of the life and teaching of the Master.

develops in disciples and the power to which they attain, in olden times periods of seclusion and vows of secrecy were arranged as part of the more deeply occult functions of the Mystery Schools. For a time the outer world of fellowmen was replaced by association with those who dwell within that inner world wherein the Greater Mysteries demand an increasing dominance. Once more, a messenger from a hierophant invited the awakened one to pass with him through the now opened doors of the temple. Strong arms were immediately outstretched in proffered aid and ungloved hands gave welcome to the new world of light into which the selfless person had found the way. These words are, however, largely figurative, because today both entrance and temple are, to use a biblical term, generally "not made with hands."[3] However, they are even more real, as the wanderer himself, now on the way "home," discovers. Visible temples, secret shrines, and places of retreat from a selfish and noisy world do exist. Nevertheless, the real doorway is within the mind of the aspirant and the sacred shrine within the heart, however solidly they appear to be represented in the world without. Although apparently withdrawn from public gaze, these institutions remain and continue to be active today in the same ways. Nowadays guidance, support during periods of strain, test, and temptation, and when possible, changes of circumstances —whether slight or considerable—take the place of admission to the temple rites of old.

In modern days, because of the phase of development upon which humanity began to embark and through which it continues to be passing—namely the unfoldment of the intellect—the required aids are directed increasingly to the thinking principle. Ancient philosophic teachings revealing eternal verities are restated, reissued as far as possible in terms likely to be comprehensible and acceptable by the developing and inquiring human mind.

Today, because the costs of living are so high, such disciples must often work for their living and therefore are able to live only a partially secluded life. While still retaining contact with the world and still keeping in touch with worldly life in a highly disciplined form, they associate largely if not entirely with fellow aspirants. Their homes become their ashrams and their "monastic cells." Their customs fo. living must be reasonably

3. 2 Cor. 5:1.

refined, a vegetarian diet and very strict conformity to the highest moral principles being examples. Inwardly, however, they are just as much as of old, members of an accepted Mystery Temple and are living in nearly every respect what may rightly be referred to as the temple life. Little if any of this is particularly apparent to their visitors and to those who study under them, even though the advanced evolutionary stature is usually recognized. Psychologically, intellectually, and spiritually, they are as much in seclusion as in olden days and in almost continuous superphysical communication with their Elders.

Occasionally words of counsel will be offered by one who has reached the position of hierophant, who in addition will silently share his attainment in the form of perceived auric powers and radiance which evoke a more deeply determined will to attain to the same position.[4] Thus, whether in privileged seclusion or in the midst of the fulfillment of duties in the outer world, the inner, the occult, the increasingly spiritualized life may be lived even while meeting the demands of duty and of karma from earlier incarnations. The danger exists that personal guidance from a Master might cause a flare-up of personal pride and self-satisfaction that could not only prevent the fulfillment of the Teacher's plan, but even mar the rest of the person's incarnation. Occult privileges, misinterpreted as indications of personal greatness and importance, not only force the Teacher to withdraw, but lead to serious self-delusions. An occult experience may, for example, be almost totally misunderstood, pridefully received, so that the recipient falls into grievous errors concerning the causes, the nature, and the sources of the experience. Delusion can then rob an individual of all benefit from the proffered aid, if only by causing the idea to arise in his mind that a system of communication from ultraplanetary and cosmic sources has been inaugurated in his special case. Unfortunately, in these days many have become victims of this delusion and in consequence have grievously misled increasing numbers of followers, themselves becoming similarly deluded. The greatest and most wise discrimination and the most intelligent evaluation of such experiences are essential to success in guiding an otherwise promising person.

---

4 .Aura (Gr. and Lat.) A subtly, physically invisible essence that emanates from human, animal, and even inanimate bodies. See Glossary.

Deep concern is felt by the adept guardians of the human race—from those who have newly attained to the very highest of all, the One Initiator[5]—for all those who might fall under the delusion of grandeur and so fail in their high endeavor. In consequence, a carefully planned protective procedure was carried out in olden days and has been continued up to the present time. The rewards to both the successful candidate and the whole of humanity were and still are so great that such care was and still is an urgent necessity. The *first* necessity in all cases of supranormal experience—if the adept Teacher's plan is to be fulfilled—is to completely dissociate all ideas of self-sufficiency, self-importance, and of being a "chosen" person, from the adeptic intervention and its possible results. A difficulty in meeting this demand arises from the fact that intellectualism can be closely associated with personal pride and what may be called "personality" in general. In the present intellectual age, pride may indeed both precede and bring about a fall. No slightest thought or assumption of superiority should exist or be displayed in contacts with fellowmen. Indeed, humility is one of the outstanding characteristics of those who succeed. This is not a falsely displayed modesty born of assumption of spiritual stature, but is based upon knowledge of one's true position on the evolutionary ladder—as yet upon the lower rungs. Above, height upon height, are those who first befriended the aspirants and afterward became their teachers, guiding them through the apparent complexities of occult science and the applications of that knowledge to daily life. Beneath them—purely in the evolutionary sense and in no way regarded as inferior—are those who later will follow after them in attempting the difficult ascent to the heights.

Undue asceticism, which would draw the attention of others, is avoided, even though a well controlled and chaste life is lived. Severe with himself, the aspirant who has advanced thus far is ever lenient toward the shortcomings of others, never demanding from them a regime which their evolutionary stature would not permit them to follow. He is quiet-spoken and accentuates the good qualities and good conduct of others rather than imputing blame. An exception to this rule concerns deliberately chosen pain-producing conduct. This could

5. Sanat Kumara (Sk.), "the eternal Virgin Youth." The head of the Occult Hierarchy of the Adepts of this planet. See *Lecture Notes of the School of the Wisdom,* Geoffrey Hodson, Vol. 1, p. 497.

never be condoned, especially when another is made to suffer for selfish gratification, cruelty, and pleasure. Very early in the great quest, such conduct comes to be regarded as abominable, such motives examples of self-degradation. He is ready to speak out strongly against grave abuses and a deliberate choice of evil conduct. Sometimes righteous indignation will burn within him like a consuming fire, and this may cause an outbreak of highly indignant censure, but even this becomes increasingly under the control of the will.

Thus, almost everyone who has reached the stage of discipleship inevitably becomes a teacher. This is his mission in life as far as contact with others is concerned. The time inevitably draws near when advice and guidance are sought by those newly awakened. Since the laws of the occult life may never with impunity be broken, he is obliged to insist that obedience to them is essential to occult development and spiritual progress. His method of teaching, however, will be far removed from preaching and almost wholly dependent upon example and the perception by students that, modest though he is, the teacher has actually advanced far beyond them. Thereafter, increasingly his counsel will be sought, accepted, and followed with gratitude. Even in Retreat, the fact becomes obvious that he is deeply engrossed with the Divine so that his life is lived in perpetual communion therewith.

Thus, the initiate-to-be moves about in the world modestly, kindly, and with a certain even, studied normality, particularly in relationships with those in whom the ideal of the path has not yet been born. A truly awakened person is one who freely gives light, life, wisdom, knowledge, encouragement, and the outstretched hand to all with whom he comes into contact. In return, he asks nothing except a certain quiet impersonality and normality in all such interrelationships. He seeks not to shine but rather to be invisible, not to be acclaimed but rather quietly to be taken for granted, his supernormal faculties being, if anything, ignored. Yet the Divine shines out in him, awakening the aspiration to enlightenment in all those who are able to perceive it.

16

Future Education for Initiation

WHILE MANKIND is passing through this present age, the stages of development from the relatively primitive to the initiated and then to the perfected Adepts greatly need to be quickened. Accentuation of scientific and other purely intellectual attainments at the present time stands in the way of the full illumination of the human intellect. This illumination occurs as a result of the functioning of the intuitive faculty but the intuition is largely prevented from operating when the concrete mind is fully active. For many, this development is already beginning to occur, if only in brief but prophetic flashes. Spiritually minded people are increasing in number.

History ever repeats itself, and although the exact methods of earlier days—the Mystery Schools—will not necessarily reappear, their spirit and general method will become increasingly apparent. Today, again and in even greater fullness, directness, and potency, the wondrous mystery ceremonials, teachings, and guidances in living a spiritual life amid the fulfillment of worldly duties are in the process of being restored. Instead of massive Egyptian, Grecian, and Roman temples with their stately ceremonials of deepening degrees of occult revelations of truth delivered to initiates, a more general spreading of the universal Wisdom will occur. The temples will be far more, though not entirely, intellectual in character and their rites less symbolic than concerned with actual occult experience. Derived from knowledge of the hidden powers, forces, and intelligences in nature and their existence and functions in man, the neophytes will in many cases be reincarnated members of ancient mystery organizations and in varying degrees prepared for direct revelation of truths concerning cosmos, man, and their interrelationships. The spread throughout the Western worlds of knowledge of the theories and practices of Eastern—but actually universal—yoga, now taking place, is one example of this tendency.

The procedure must, perforce, be quite gradual, if only because whenever ritual initiations are performed added power is likely to be bestowed upon the outer personality of recipients. Because of the vicious tendencies yet remaining in the nature of the candidates, such vices as hate, anger, and their expression as cruelty, may become more difficult to eradicate. Hence those privileged to be recipients of spiritual quickening must be carefully chosen. Humanity, then, must still further cleanse itself of these attributes of human temperament. Wars must cease, and disputes—whether national or personal—must increasingly be solved and settled by means of degrees of surrender and the acceptance and application of persuasiveness in the highest meaning of that word.

In the epoch of human life and development now being entered, a new form of education for young people, which might be called education for disciples and initiates, will have to be instituted. The time must therefore come when educational systems and institutions are based upon recognition of the possibility that scholars of both sexes may be naturally imbued with a call to the religious life and an aspiration to concentrate their studies upon appropriate subjects and pursuits. The whole world, but more especially the so-called Middle Eastern and the total Western world, greatly needs to be prepared for the arrival into families, and so into schools and universities, of young people who do not happily or usefully fit into materially oriented curricula and out-of-classroom occupations.

At the same time, neither authorities nor students should suggest that they or their ways of life are superior to those of their fellows. They will be regarded as different, of course, and arrangements will have to be made so that they can pursue their own ideals and ways of life in perfect freedom and without interference by the staff or the other scholars. Ultimately, it may be assumed, whole schools will come into existence with no other purposes than education for idealists of all ages. Needless to say, teachers imbued with the same ideals, experiencing the same aspirations and inspired by the same purposes for living, will need to be found. Reincarnated yogis, idealists, disciples of Adepts and initiates in the mystery tradition, will naturally respond to the purposes of such educational systems. They will form the personnel of both the students who attend the classes and the teachers who direct and instruct. As the state of the world and the conditions of human life upon it gradually improve from the point of view of international relationships and world peace, so—it may be expected—will increasing numbers of young people become capable of favorable reactions to such organizations.

The age at which people experience and respond to idealistic tendencies from former lives differs greatly. As in the case of youthful prodigies, some respond consciously or in the natural display of faculty when very young. Others, however, may not experience the pull toward the spiritual way of living and the ideal of service until the late teens or even still later in life. Many factors are involved in these variations and include conditions of home life, early schooling, world conditions—especially peace or war—into which they are born.

Traditionally the age at which spiritual urges become decisive and overpoweringly demanding is between twenty-eight and thirty-three in the case of males and rather earlier in the case of females, though of course variations occur. Admittedly, ways other than specialized schools for encouraging and helping older aspirants will need to be found as a more evolved humanity than the present comes into incarnation. Thus a new principle for education is needed. It includes modes of living, education, and religion designed to welcome, encourage, and in every way to assist all those who genuinely determine upon the spiritual way of life. It will include every necessity for efficient education and development from youth to manhood. In addition, teaching and training in both the mystical and the practical fulfillment of the purposes for human existence would be parts of this curriculum. These latter will need to be stated, and such pronouncements must include the following theosophical teaching concerning the constitution of man:

Man is that being in whom highest spirit (Monad) and lowest matter (body) are united by intellect.

Man's spiritual Self (Monad) perpetually unfolds potential capacities, this being the purpose for his existence.

91

This process culminates in the attainment of perfected manhood, adeptship.

The method of human evolution is by means of successive lives, or rebirth.

Human conditions and experiences are the results of human conduct under the law of cause and effect or karma. Kindness brings health and happiness. Cruelty brings disease and misery.

The processes of evolution can be hastened. The "Kingdom of Heaven" can be taken by storm. This calls for self-training, regular meditation, and selfless service.

Century by century perfect men and women arise, the rare flowering of the human race. Adepts have long existed on earth.

Ages ago, and ever since, certain Adepts have shared their discovered wisdom and knowledge with humanity. This is named *Brahma Vidya* (Sanskrit), *Theosophia* (Greek), Theosophy in modern terms.

At the heart of the activities of homes, schools, universities, and communities of older people based on these principles, there will be acceptance of two mandatory aims: the attainment of spiritual realization or realized oneness, and selfless service for the improvement of the lot of one's fellow human beings. Without these two, now and forever, all proclamations of idealism will prove to be futile so far as their fruits are concerned. All who would respond to the call to the heights must direct their total energy, capacity, and interest with these two purposes in view; the great Teachers who became founders or inspirers of existing religions throughout their lives stressed their importance and illustrated their acceptance and application. These ideals would produce inspired directors and teachers who by virtue of their own knowledge could in turn lead humanity toward the living heart of all religion, namely experienced oneness with the Divine and its expression by means of wisely directed, loving service. If humanity is to be led toward that spiritual ideal and practice from which alone mankind may progress into an era of world brotherhood, then it is essential that a beginning be made with youth.

The schools of the future, as also colleges and universities, must of necessity turn the minds of their scholars and students toward the idealism here put forward: for they in their turn will in consequence be moved and enabled to bring about that world reform by which mankind may be saved from itself.

Education must become one with the religious life. A new definition of religion[1] is greatly needed and may thus be brought about through the medium of education. Divine worship in its reality must gradually cease to be thought of and practiced as largely, if not entirely, going to church. Church worship does have its spiritually elevating and inspiring place in man's inner life. When, however, it is regarded too much as a necessary conformity and too little as a communion with one's own divine Self, it can lull a person into an unconsidered misbelief that church attendance is more important than inwardly experienced communion with God.

Unhappily, the spiritual and the practical hearts of each of the world faiths have become overlaid by accentuation of the external acts, ceremonials and more worldly proclamations and objectives. Ceremonies and ceremonial practices can be useful aids both in attaining to these interior illuminations and as directives concerning the practice of spiritual idealism in daily life. The danger is that ceremonies and the traditional customs disproportionately assume predominance. Furthermore, instead of a world-wide mystery temple life, made available to those who seek with pure hearts and regulated minds to find and enter it, religious antagonisms and narrow sectarian divisions are found. These, together with the difficulties referred to, delay the reestablishment on earth of a unified school and temple procedure for training in the spiritual life. The real purpose for the existence of world faiths—the discovery of the presence of God both outside and within—may find little or no place either in the performance of religious ceremonies or attendance at them.

A change is needed so that contemplation of the Divine will have its daily place in one's religious life. Church worship would then be regarded as a means of attaining to realization of union with God. Certain practices derived from and in continuance of the methods of Ancient Mysteries, can prove to be very helpful, especially for those unable to comprehend

1. Religion, Latin *religere:* to bind back.

more subtle philosophic ideas. By such methods these may inwardly enter into realization of such eternal verities as the omnipresence of the one divine Life throughout all nature and know by direct experience that the same Divinity lives and moves within themselves.

Thus, a balance is needed between full retreat from the active into the contemplative life on the one hand, and church-going alone, on the other—though each is worthy of respect. Human temperament must, of course, be granted its due recognition in such evaluations, since human beings differ by nature in their needs for and responses to various forms of religion. Some people, for example, will find exhilaration and upliftment in beautifully presented and performed religious ceremonial. Others, however, may find this to be a distraction of the mind and heart from the inward communion which they seek. There are those for whom beauty is seen as another name for God. Appreciation and expression of beauty in the arts and in one's surrounding is for them as much a true religion as going to church. Others will consider religion to be discovery of Reality, particularly when sought and achieved by penetration beyond illusion into truths themselves. The eternal verity that stands revealed by this process is a manifestation of the Divine, and its discovery by and within the mind is a form of religious service and fulfillment. For such people as these, God is simply Truth, and contemplation consists of intellectual and intuitive search.

One of the purposes for which the Theosophical Movement was initiated was to provide a somewhat centralized system of guidance in the mystical and occult life. This has been partly achieved in the first century of its existence. Indeed, The Theosophical Society through its members has performed splendid work during the first hundred years of its life in effectively presenting the basic teachings of Theosophy to mankind. This, one may be assured, The Theosophical Society will continue to do.

An extension of the work of the Society into this more specialized field may well at this present time receive consideration. In addition to the founding of sections and branches, groups might form for purposes of what might be called "the temple life." A worldwide meditation and contemplation organization might usefully be founded, unifying separate groups and granting freedom to each. If this is not done, separation among groups that do not readily combine have the effect of delaying the reestablishment and growth of a modern mystery foundation for all mankind.

This movement, if successful, could not only prove very helpful for all true seekers for the inward light—reincarnated members of the Ancient Mysteries, as some of them are—but also lead gradually and naturally to the establishment of what might perhaps be called *the mystery method.* Such a carefully, wisely organized, movement would lead to stages of progress through the degrees of probation, discipleship, initiation, and eventually Adeptship. Presumably, those who responded and gained admittance would be people who had heard and answered the call to the heights.

In the days of the Ancient Mysteries, Adept guidance was available—Imhotep and Hermes Trismegistus, as possible examples—in the founding and direction of the activities of the greater temples of Egypt, Greece, and other lands. Would it be too presumptuous, one might ask, to hope for a reinstitution in more modern forms of this Mahatmic guidance? Whether visibly or invisibly, such perfect instruction in the establishment of methods of study, meditation, and the application of their fruits to daily life would then be available. The Theosophical Society as originally planned and since developing, is one example of Adept-inspired activity. There will undoubtedly be secluded centers. People of like minds will gather together, often far away from city life and even country townships. This will ensure that reasonably "virginal" psychic and intellectual privacy and purity are available. These specialized conditions are essential to the development of the intuitive faculty and to the rule of spirituality over physical, emotional, and mental modes of living. The "hierophants" of the future will be manifestations of spiritual will within vehicles of the purest, clearest intuitive insight. The touch of the thyrsus will then be represented by, and experienced as, radiant flashes of direct knowledge.[2] This may quite often prove to be incommunicable, if only because far subtler than any possible verbal communication in intellectual terms. It will also be especially pertinent to each recipient, by whom it will be treasured within the silence of the heart.

Meanwhile, the continual popularization of the Wisdom of

---

2. Thyrsus—Hierophantic staff or rod of power.

the Ages must ever be the foundation for all such temples not made with hands. Those who would assist in this entry —reentry in many cases—of mankind into the Mystery Religion, cannot possibly do better than first master, then apply to their own lives, and thereafter make available to inquirers, that *Theosophia* which is truly named *Divine Wisdom*. Here is the call. Such is the opportunity. Much of the Wisdom has already been reintroduced into human thought, emotion, and worldly life. It will be almost self-revealed as it were, to present and succeeding races.

Such is the possibility now opening before mankind. This is partly evidenced by the founding of The Theosophical Society as one result of the pronouncement by H. P. Blavatsky of the existence on earth of great Adepts who were personally known to her. The increasing numbers of yoga and meditation groups now being formed attracting young and old draw attention to this possibility and support the idea of an appropriate worldwide movement. By such means and doubtless by many others, the pathway to the interior light may become increasingly discovered and opened to the mystical and seriously seeking aspirants.

17

The Most Serious Fall

THE IMMENSELY IMPORTANT and significant decision to enter upon the path of hastened progress to human perfection is the product of the advanced evolutionary stature of the reincarnating Self; for with this decision is born a hitherto dormant spiritual attribute. When this awakens it always takes the same form—the decision to seek, find, and tread the path of discipleship. The methods of its expression vary according to such influences as the ascendancy of one or other of the seven rays active in the present personality. The predominant effect is, however, discernible as an increase in willpower and its determined application to exclusive preoccupation with reaching the goal of human evolution as quickly as possible. Whatever the ray, upbringing, education, life experiences, social condition, environment and, of course, health, this interiorly impelling decision more and more determines the motive for almost every action.

The degree, nature, and especially persistence of response to this inward decision are of very great importance. Further guidance may be added on the subject of dangers and falls for every aspirant to the spiritual heights. Most important is the spirit in which the attempt is begun, the strength of the aspiration, and persistence even when aspiration tends to become reduced or even for a time to seem to die away. The path is too steep, it may be thought, the ground too difficult, the height too great, the longing for the accustomed comforts and pleasures of a wordly life too strong. All of these lags and others can assail the inward spirit and enthusiasm, the keenness, and even the desire for attainment. However much the spiritual "feet" may drag, slowing or temporarily holding up the ascent, the aspirant must never admit defeat. Those who have attained the summit advise those who have not yet become Ego-ruled to continue, continue, keep on at all costs. Constant permission should be granted to the will to direct, if not wholly to control, thought and conduct once the interior awakening has been rationalized and consciously put into action. While the degree of dominance of this decision will vary, it is of almost incalculable importance to understand and remember.

The endeavor to reach the spiritual heights rapidly is *always* undertaken on behalf of the indwelling Life evolving on earth. As stated before, this is because the very Life-Essence in the aspiring soul is identical with that in every other being throughout all the kingdoms of nature. True, the personality may not immediately be wholly aware of this extremely intimate interrelationship and continuous interaction and does not accept responsibility, particularly at the level of the formal mind. Nevertheless, a pledge has been physically repeated in which the whole nature of the disciple and the evolving Life in all forms is very deeply concerned, far more deeply in fact, than is at first generally realized. To break that pledge and to engage in conduct which positively contravenes the rules of the spiritual life are errors, the seriousness of which is grievous indeed. Hence this warning which may at first appear to be overemphasized.

All such responsibility has been voluntarily assumed by highly privileged disciples of an adept Teacher; for they themselves sought out that Teacher and pledged themselves faithfully to behave as disciples. Even in the conduct of the affairs of the worldly life—business for example—honor, honesty, and the faithful adherence to rules of the inner life are regarded as essentials. Far more, however, do they apply to the morality of the relationship between a human being and a member of the Adept Hierarchy.

When a person deliberately and without due thought of the consequences—especially broken vows—gives up the whole enterprise of endeavoring to quicken the rate of evolutionary development for the sake of all mankind, he becomes traitorous. Such faithfulness applies not only in reference to the relationship between the outer man and the inner Self, but to that between disciple and Master, and also between that disciple and all his or her fellowmen.

To turn against the great ideal is tantamount to flouting the will of God. The deliberate turning of one's back upon the whole idealism of the quest and a self-chosen return to indulgences are certain to prove disastrous. A self-chosen surrender to temptations and the appearance of an almost defiant attitude toward, and adverse speech concerning the path —these are so very harmful, both to the one thus falling and to all who are affected thereby.

Rest from spiritual and occult endeavors, particularly those of the more intense forms, is perfectly permissible. A quiet retreat from external activities due to a sense of overstrain and fatigue is indeed not only permissible but a wise choice, as little or no harm is done to anyone. Physical breakdown can mar the whole procedure, not only for the aspirant but in the eyes of those neophytes who might not understand the delicate issues involved. Flagrant breaking of the rules, denial of ideals, and—still more serious—invective against fellow-travelers and leaders on the upward path must be avoided. This book would fail of its purpose and prove unworthy were these statements not included. This is not only for its own sake or the moral issue, but also because of the potentially long-term harmful effects in the same life and those which immediately follow.

Such falls have either formed part of one's earlier life or have newly presented themselves as means of sensual gratification and physical pleasure. When once one has taken even the early steps on the self-chosen upward path, then he must neither look back nor go back, as the story of Lot's wife indicates.[1] When a person does again thus fall by continuing to direct attention to material goals; to assume old and undesirable habits of body; to take pleasure in uncontrolled, sensual emotions and selfish, possessive, prideful thinking; then inevitably a curtain or veil is drawn across the hitherto gradually thinning barrier between the higher and lower minds. The *antahkarana*, the path or bridge between the higher, abstract intelligence and the lower, formal mind, becomes closed, thereby shutting off communication between the immortal spiritual soul and the mortal personal man.

One such effect of this is a deadening while physically awake, a certain loss of personal responsiveness to the inspiring enlightening, and empowering influence of the interior Self.

1. Gen. 18:26, to be read as an allegory.

The Monad-Ego then loses a large measure of its power over the personality of the individual. However, while nature's rules concerning success in self-spiritualization are in themselves rigid, obedience to them—particularly by a so-called man or woman of the world—may prove to be somewhat gradual. When the determination to proceed despite all obstacles is still the accepted decision, it is possible to recover from slips, stumbles, and unplanned falls. However, every time aspirants *deliberately* turn their eyes in a direction known to be the opposite of the ideal attitude, they both weaken their powers of achievement and slow down their spiritual progress.

Fortunately, such falls are not irrevocable. Other lives will follow in which the ideals of the spiritual life may again be accepted and successfully applied as "Rules of the Road." Helping hands are always available, both to prevent or soften the impact of falls and to assist in recovery, that is unless, tragically, the self-darkening decision has become final.

However, although aspirants continue to appear in these times in increasing numbers, such falls are few. The purpose for these chapters of warning is to save those who step forward from the ranks from such mistakes, to warn and to guide them. A deliberate recourse to evil and the darker magic is of course far more serious, but need hardly be discussed here, if only because of obviousness.

The wave of spiritual inspiration is tidal. It may ebb and flow. Personal circumstances and astrological influences play their part. Every aspirant should be on guard and in thought and meditation establish an unalterable determination that such return to past modes of living will never, must never, occur. By this practice, a form of *self-guardianship* becomes established. Then, for personal instruction and always with complete detachment, the life stories and the living examples of those who are known to have given up the path ideal as a standard of thinking and living should be studied. By such means, self-education may be drawn from life itself. "Onward and ever-upward," as if by habit, becomes the life-motive after the call has been heard and answered. Indeed, it is the very theme of the thought processes of those who—for the sake of maximum efficiency in the service of their fellowmen—would as quickly as possible reach the goal described by St. Paul as "the measure of the stature of the fullness of Christ."[2]

2. Eph. 4:13.

Such indeed, is the ever-absorbing ideal which increasingly assumes control of the personal thinking and living of the aspirant who, in the words of Brother Lawrence "is possessed by the gale of the Holy Spirit"; for indeed, it is true that he "goes forward even in sleep."[3]

3. Brother Lawrence, *The Practice of the Presence of God.*

18

Pitfalls

ESTABLISHING PREDOMINATING claims is of very great significance to every human being who embarks upon the pathway of self-discovery, spiritual self-expression, and service to others. He or she needs to be continually watchful lest former interests and modes of life force into the background of consciousness the awakening spirituality and its idealistic effects upon mind, emotion, and mode of life. Watchfulness thus becomes a word of great importance to all neophytes as they respond to the interior impulse. At first, this may not be strong, but it eventually leads to a radical change of both motive for living and mode of life. Until the reign of spiritual Self over mortal man—especially bodily man—is completely established, revolutionary changes in different ways for differing temperaments are prone to evoke resistance. This may be experienced psychologically or mentally as a change of heart; or karma may precipitate an enforced and irresistible change in bodily life, in health, work, or personal acquaintances, or a serious temptation which tests the pupil in one or another of his more vulnerable parts. Obstacles are inevitable in fulfilling the spiritual ideal that includes forcing the evolutionary pace beyond the normal speed. This is because the past still weighs heavily upon both the present and the future. Habit, the demands of physical life and its relationships, interest in the phenomena amid which one lives, all tend to distract attention. These claim and imprison interest in a mode of life in which self has been at the center and from there makes predominating claims.

The physical body and its intimately associated elemental tendencies has—usefully indeed—become a being of customary activities. These—which had been built in, as it were, by their continuous application to a customary way of life from waking in the morning to sleeping at night—are not readily relinquished, particularly at the beginning of the great quest. In addition, there are elements called in Sanskrit *skandhas,*[1] meaning in this sense qualities and attributes of the substances of which the mental, emotional, and physical bodies are built. Inherent as a result of racial habits and indulgences, certain of these tendencies which may have been inactive earlier may now become active or awakened with a peculiar force. An aspirant may not be wholly prepared for this, as it is unsuspected, and in consequence may become distracted from the great ideal, slip into indulgence, be moved by pride, possessiveness, sensuality, or even sheer greed.

Falls may occur, whether affecting the remainder of the physical life or being but temporary. Needless to say, they should be guarded against as invulnerably as possible and, if they occur, recovery must be made quickly and even enforcedly. Those who aspire directly to discover and understand the *Gnosis* or Truth itself must persist in their endeavors, however loudly what is not inappropriately named "the world, the flesh and the devil" may call. A tragic failure is exemplified by Judas Iscariot who fell below the ideal of the pursuit of perfection under an adept Teacher.[2] Judas fell prey to the twin lures of praise by authorities and favored position on the one hand, and of the greed for money on the other. The desire to be popular and the weakness of cupidity brought about his downfall for that life, allegorically represented by his suicide.[3] A particular fall, or tendency thereto, consists of an at first unrealized development of self-will. Spiritual will-force becomes so strong as to produce the danger of imbalance in the personal character of the disciple. Indeed, this may become so obsessive as to render him unresponsive to—even unconscious of—either his own inward voice of conscience or that of his Teacher. This is one of the greatest perils to be met with on the path of swift unfoldment. A hitherto malleable and reasonable person can develop into a self-appointed superior who may demand obedience to his orders from collaborators and others.

1. Skandhas (Sk.)—see Glossary.
2. Matt. 26:14.
3. Matt. 27:5.

The pride of personal power can also result from superiority of intellect and the added knowledge this bestows. Intellectual development, which also occurs under the adept Master's influence, may induce in the formal mind and physical personality of the disciple, an overaccentuation of the analytical mind as applied to life's problems, so that the appraisal of relative values can become *very* erroneous. The formal intelligence then tends to become the test—acid test in fact—causing harsh criticisms and judgments and an insistence that such assessments are the only true ones and must be obeyed. Here, the occult axiom most especially applies, "The mind is the great slayer of the Real. Let the disciple slay the slayer."[4] All aspirants should continually be on guard against the grave mistake of overconfidence, self-aggrandizement, and self-will. In a word, *pride* is one of the most serious pitfalls upon the path.

Another difficulty consists of previously habitual concern as to how one's life will look to other people. This can indeed be a serious obstacle, since embarkation upon an increasingly spiritual way of life while still living in the world may cause one to be eyed askance by those who are as yet not similarly awakened. Such people are naturally obedient to rules and formalities as to how human beings should conduct themselves before their fellowmen. It is at this point that either temporary or complete withdrawal from the world may be necessary. The esoteric life may seem a somewhat lonely venture. Actually, the fully awakened aspirant becomes less and less affected by worldly standards and those who follow them, correct as they may be for worldly minded people.

Another and quite different kind of error arises from a deepening intuitive awareness of the bond of unity which intimately relates all beings, so that oneness is realized. Such experiences occur during meditation and in flashes of intuited identity between one's own life and that in other manifestations in the human and subhuman kingdoms. This development, valuable and important as it is, needs to be understood and very wisely directed. Otherwise, a thus unified person may become overly susceptible to personal love and the receipt of love from others. This can lead to undesirable attachments, sensuality, and experiences which can gravely delay, and even prevent for that particular life, otherwise promising progress toward the goal of adeptship.

4. *The Voice of the Silence,* H. P. Blavatsky.

Such impediments as pride demanding implicit obedience, sensuality, and undesirable attachments, harsh criticisms and tyrannical judgments, along with an unconscious self-praise, can erect a shell around the disciple. These mistakes tend to produce a kind of exclusiveness, applied not only to fellow human beings but even to the Master. The disciple should be ever on the watch against falling into this error. Obviously, practices and indulgences must be totally excluded which of themselves may anaesthetize the mind in the brain and, as a result of excesses, cause that organ to become occultly and spiritually unresponsive. All mind-bedulling food, drink, and drugs (medical prescriptions apart) must be avoided, and this avoidance must become an overwhelming, overriding and decisive bodily rule. The enjoyment of pleasure-giving drugs—smoking and cannabis for example—must cease, because they dull those areas of the brain in which impluses and directions from the interior Self are received. These include the pituitary and pineal glands, with surrounding parts of the brain, and the thalamus. Any conduct whatever which reduces the spiritual responsiveness of the brain must cease, the sooner the better, once the inward call has been heard and answered affirmatively. In addition, the intake of stimulants must be reduced to a minimum and eventually cease, especially alcohol and mind-expanding drugs.

Modern man has employed his increasing mental capacities to the end of discovering secrets concerning natural products and their effects upon his body. These effects can be both helpful and harmful, their results sometimes extreme in either direction. Remedial drugs and other natural products are of course very beneficial and their discovery must therefore be regarded as highly praiseworthy. Unfortunately, misuse, including excessive use, renders these agencies potentially harmful to the body, to the mind-brain, and to the incarnated dweller in them both. This is especially apparent whenever a spiritually awakening, partly awakened or—tragically indeed—a fully awakened person falls into bedulling practices. This error hardly needs further statement or exposition; for the whole aim of the contemplative life is the attainment of continually increasing responsiveness to the Self within. Contemplation in quietude, meditative considerations of abstract ideas experienced as veritable truths, the utterance of prayers and the chanting of mantras,[5] however earnest, sincere, and correctly performed, will inevitably fail if one who practices them does so with a drug-bedulled brain. How can delicately quietened music, a soft sweet voice, the approach of a hoped-for footstep be heard if the organ of hearing has been reduced in its capacity to respond to the more refined sounds? If a healthful regimen is not followed, then all the yoga in the world will fail of its objective of realized identity with that nameless Spirit Essence which is, however, referred to as the One Alone.

Every normally intelligent individual will understand and respond to these very obvious instructions. They are included in this work in order that guidance along the inward pathway may be as complete, full, and protective as possible. The history of the Mystery Tradition contains accounts of those falls here being referred to that have tragically brought to an end—at least for the period of the life in question—all hopes of further progress toward the Holy of Holies, access thereto, and final mergence within. Hence, these warning words.

Distraction is another serious menace which besets every aspirant. Modern man living in the modern world has constructed himself a veritable mountain of distractions. This situation may be regarded as typical of an age such as the present in which mankind has become increasingly mind-ruled. Conveniences for travel over distances which may be either short or long, communications which may be local or worldwide, continual attention drawn by the press to news near and far, and the innumerable forms of entertainment in the home and beyond—these, together with the demands of the necessities of life, render persistent response to the inward Call extremely difficult. In consequence, the voice of the soul is but dimly heard at first amid worldly distractions. It loses much of its power to control the thinking and conduct of a person who is habituated to and largely controlled by personal, domestic, civic, national, and international events and crises.

How, then, is the awakening human being to respond fully to the inward Call amid these ever-mounting distractions? The suggested answer, as earlier described, includes regular daily prayer, meditation, contemplation of both divine truths and

5. Mantra (Sk., speech). A form of words or syllables rhythmically arranged so that when sounded certain vibrations are generated, producing a desired effect on higher planes.

the divine Presence within all that exists—to the end of experienced oneness therewith. These are the safeguards and the sources of power to mind and heart by which the aspirant may achieve a firm footing upon the upward way. Fortunately, both instinct and interest tend to beckon in these directions. In addition, and equally—if not more—important, there should be formed the habit of will-empowered resistance to everything outside of the demands of duty, especially that which accentuates interest in the transient and the impermanent. The Eternal should—and one day *will* —increasingly absorb mind, heart and interests. Indeed, the permanent must call with ever-growing power, until that which is truly everlasting alone has power to grip and to hold the attention—external and inward—of the awakening wanderer amid the pitfalls and dangers of the worldly life.

This and other actions of self-discipline will be difficult or easy and natural according to progress made in former lives in the direction of the attainment of complete self-command. Success in recovery from a fall depends upon such factors as the degree of self-degradation and the extent to which the choice was either deliberate, for the sake of gratification or a failure because the strain became too much, bodily life and circumstances overcoming the aspirant's willpower. Temptation must be included, particularly that carried out either by a seducer acting for pleasure's sake or an agent of the Powers of Darkness.

In the latter case obstruction on the path may have been engineered—or taken advantage of—by the class of entities in whom the forces and tendencies toward destruction are in control. Information about these may be thought of as a branch of the tree of Occult Science dealing with particular forces and entities that are "opposites." Unless neophytes find themselves confronted, attacked, or disoriented mentally by such beings, their existence should be entirely ignored—academic occultism apart. Indeed, the aspirant is advised to turn his or her back upon, to exclude from thought, all such entities. When, however, the more advanced grades of the Mysteries have been passed and the required instruction has been imparted to the initiate, the power and knowledge to safeguard others effectively from such adverse agencies may permissibly be used for self-protection. The adept Master will be aware of any such emergencies and will awaken in, and bestow upon, the disciple that degree of spiritual force (Atma) that will enable him to deal with such situations. Until the stature of adeptship has been attained, no human being is entirely free of what might be called "oppositeness." Matter itself, at the present stage of evolution, is as yet far from being wholly free from what might perhaps be described as the pull of earthiness. In consequence, the mortal part of man, built of such coarse matter, is by no means immune from either grossly material inner tendencies or the influences of grossness tempting him from without.

A battle begins to be waged, as it were, between the past and its demands and the future with its appeal which at first is intermittent. To deny or shut out the call, to shrug off the increasing tendencies to a cleaner, healthier, and more beautiful way of life, and to continue as before is a temptation—the real "temptation in the wilderness"[6]—against which neophytes must ever be on guard. This is part of the so-called warfare, the battle waged on the field of *Kurukshetra* that is above all an interior, psychological conflict.[7] Admittedly, all such wars are scripturally and mythologically portrayed as external battles between those who represent opposing influences and objectives. Nevertheless, the real "wars in heaven," such as conflicts between heroes and their enemies, are susceptible of interpretation as Myths. They are allegorically descriptive of the various forms in which the refining tendencies and the materializing influences wage war against each other—in fact an actuality. The aspirant has voluntarily engaged upon a veritable fight in which the habits and customs of almost the whole world of fellowmen are arrayed against him. It is clear, is it not, that everyone who challenges the rhythms of nature, including the speed of normal progressions, David-like must stand alone before Goliath and conquer or fail in each particular battle. The story is particularly applicable to deliberately chosen self-quickening and to the power and capacity for victory represented by the slings and stones with which the Davids of the world are self-equipped.

The battle will be won in the end, but victory may be hastened or delayed by the manner in which from the very first a spiritually awakening person responds to the inward call. An aspirant may well at first shrink from such a change knowing

6. Matt. 4:1-11.
7. *Kurukshetra*—Battlefield in which events in the *Bhagavad Gita* took place.

that it will be revolutionary. Ultimately, the forces in human nature between which a veritable war is being waged alter in "numbers" and "armaments," as it were; for inevitably the past loses its power and so its grip upon the present, while the future grows in effectiveness at every level. Gradually, intellectual, philosophical, and spiritual aspirations become so strong as almost of themselves to bring about a cessation of surrender to undesirable habits. Nevertheless, aid is ever available, chiefly in the form of inspiration, instruction in general, and guidance on particular occasions. Even though no particular Adept or human senior may be known to be watching, nevertheless watchful care is continually maintained by appointed seniors. Without undue penetration into the privacy of the individual, the general state and the degree of progress are benignly observed.

A pupil of an adept Master, advanced disciple and initiate of the Greater Mysteries, will experience an increase of strength of purpose, determination to proceed for the sake of fellow human beings. Capacity to continue until the so-called weaknesses of human nature are entirely outgrown will increase. Nevertheless, the above-mentioned dangers will continue to exist.

The necessary ideals are clearly and beautifully summed up in the statement by H. P. Blavatsky known as "The Golden Stairs."

A clean life, an open mind, a pure heart, an eager intellect, an unveiled spiritual perception, a courageous endurance of personal injustice, a brave declaration of principles, a valiant defence of those who are unjustly attacked, and a constant eye to the ideal of human progression and perfection which the Sacred Science depicts—these are the golden stairs up the steps of which the learner may climb to the Temple of Divine Widsom.

19

Safeguards

NEEDLESS TO SAY, the more evolved the reincarnating Ego, the less the likelihood of a personal fall—whether temporary or enduring—and the more rapid the recovery should one occur. Ego-ruled, the mortal man or woman who has found and successfully begun to tread the steep path usually finds himself driven—in the right meaning of that word—by an almost overmastering determination to succeed. The demand of the awakened interior Self brooks no denial. In order to "cheat" time, a kind of "spiritual impatience" must be regularly and reasonably—almost scientifically—applied to daily habits. However, expressions of these ideals are not expected to be sudden, save in those in whom they were ruling principles in former lives. Advance must be always with wisdom, meaning never too fast, never too slowly, and always with watchful care over one's mental, emotional, and physical welfare, including health. Sanity, good sense, and reasonableness are the completely essential guidelines which must be followed every step of the way.

The aspirant may become illumined during states of psychological and spiritual upliftment. These two influences tend to keep the attention away from unspiritual thinking and emotions, physical interests and experiences. In consequence, temptations are greatly reduced if they occur at all. Material achievements and temporary happinesses lose their flavor and fade away almost on the threshold of their acceptance, proving to be without any permanent satisfaction whatever. Other gratifications for oneself alone lose their significance for one whose consciousness is becoming blended with that of all human and subhuman beings. Only those attainments which benefit the whole are then acceptable, all others being not only tasteless but distasteful, since limited to a single personality. In addition, a system of self-discipline has generally been discovered and accepted; if successfully followed, this holds the feet firmly upon the narrow way. From rising in the morning to retiring at night, such an individual maintains a certain watchfulness or self-guardianship. In due course, one part of his mind becomes established in—never leaves, indeed—the contemplation of both *Theosophia* in general and the ideals of the spiritual way of life in particular.

Consideration is now given to ways by which the ideal attitude and conduct may become habitual and may be recovered by self-correction after falls that can still occur. Here are some steps to be taken by the aspiring neophyte, and those more advanced, to bring about recovery from major and minor falls.

1. The aspirant should conduct a careful and dispassionate self-examination in search of the flaws in character from which the falls have arisen.

2. Having discovered these, he should note those that are deep-seated and therefore demand radical extirpation. Those which have resulted from carelessness, "unwatchfulness" and so have led to error, must also receive careful attention. Many mistakes can arise almost heedlessly or simply by pursuing what has hitherto been natural and permissible; hence the necessity for vigilance.

3. If faults are deep-seated, then a dispassionate examination of one's whole nature must be undertaken, founded upon sincere regret and perhaps shame. More especially, motives of self-gain, remaining from earlier modes of life in which they were permissible and even necessary, must be finally eliminated.

4. The conduct under consideration should be examined to its very root until its deep-seated *cause* comes to light. This is a very important procedure.

5. Having discovered the true cause, the aspirant should maintain maximum concentration (never light or casual) upon the virtue or quality that *should* have governed motive and conduct and would have prevented the misconduct.

111

6. The time required to eradicate the "weed" will depend largely upon the degree of self-commitment, determination, and continued application of the above-described procedure. Ideally these should be of great intensity and, as far as possible, steadily maintained, the ideal or virtue being dwelt upon almost continuously, as far as other duties permit. By this method, relatively small faults and short "falls" will quickly be outgrown. More deeply seated errors in character and conduct will naturally demand closer attention and their opposite virtues concentrated upon for a longer time.

7. A somewhat subtle factor contributes to the speed at which the error may be eradicated and the ease by which complete cure without repetition may be attained. This factor concerns the intensity and genuineness of regret produced by the fall. Not only must the mistake be recognized, admitted, and faced, but deeply regretted even to a sense of shame. This may result from the fall having become known by others; or one may be painfully ashamed of oneself. Either of these experiences rightly received should lead to a manly and a frontal attack upon the weakness of character. This praiseworthy self-shame should be as reasoned and logical as possible; for then and then only may the mental cure be effectively applied.

In all other aspects of life on the Path, forgetfulness of self should reign. Even while conscious of regret and shame, the aspirant should have a balanced mental attitude. Since aspirants are still human, errors are inevitable. Faultlessness is achieved only by the Adept, not only in his perfected consciousness, but also when functioning in his physical personality.

The regular practice of prayer, religious study and ceremonial, meditative contemplation of union with God—these are not only most beneficial in themselves, but sensitize the mind and brain, rendering them increasingly responsive to what is described as spiritual grace. Regular daily meditation is of special importance. From the beginning of the attempt, a physically convenient and intellectually acceptable and suitable form of meditative contemplation should be maintained day by day. This practice must be continued even though rather artificially on some occasions, when the heart may have gone out of the whole quest. Such resistance is almost certain, though to an increasingly lesser extent for those who have begun and made progress upon the spiritual path throughout former lives.

One part of the value of regular, daily meditation—ideally to be undertaken as early as possible after response to the interior call and pursuit of the great quest—is to assist in making the change from motives of self to motives of selfless service to others. Regular inward thinking and spiritual self-discovery draw attention to the very great importance of the mystic experience induced and entered into during meditation. This results not only in directly illuminated mental experiences —valuable though these are—but in almost automatic adoption of selflessness in the conduct of life. This change comes about from spoken and literary guidance and from the examples of others and even more potently and enduringly, in response to the deepening experience of unity with the life in all other beings. Selfishness and purely selfish motives then naturally decline in their power to affect purposes for conduct, and so conduct itself. Though the necessities for living must be provided—unless one completely withdraws into a spiritual community—all conduct is increasingly idealistic, the welfare of others being the overriding purpose for virtually everything done. Once this is achieved, and becomes perfectly natural, the dangers referred to in the chapters concerned with pitfalls are reduced to a minimum; for while misjudgments may still be possible, the motives of self-gain are reduced to insignificance in the life and character of the aspirant. Then, and perhaps not till then, all obstacles are overcome, all enticements fail. Even the wishes of the most loved, such as the members of the family, can no longer be granted unless they permit—as is hardly conceivable—the pursuit of a way of life totally dedicated to the welfare of all that exists.

In addition to the maintenance of the meditative practice—"muscle building" as it is—the already voluntarily accepted disciplines for purification also need to be sustained. Even though the heart does at times weaken, the body should not be allowed to do so because bodily excesses and brain-bedulling conduct tempt one to falls. Since the body is both shrine and prison, its daily care and the maintenance of health become particularly important in the spiritual life. The body serves as a shrine for the divinity inhabiting it throughout each earthly life, for which it is also the means of approach. Spiritual will as well as thought-power must be employed if the approach to the spirit within is to be successful. Nevertheless, it is that portion of the mind that is incarnate in and employs the brain cells during waking hours which leads the wide-awake thinker into the light radiating from the Presence within. If the brain becomes dull by ill health, lack of sleep, deficient nutrition, inadequate bodily purity and cleanliness, then the mind can by no means become illumined by that light with which his true Self is so brilliantly radiant. Under these conditions the body can be a prison indeed. Therefore, when the call to the heights has been heard and is being answered, reasonable care must be granted for the provision of these necessities. Without them only a bedulled illumination is experienced, if any understandable inspiration may be received at all.

When a habitual mode of conduct contravenes the established rules and modes of living associated with self-spiritualization—those which *coarsen* the body and reduce its responsiveness to idealism—such behavior must not only cease but be reversed. In addition, degrading conduct designed to give selfish pleasure such as gratification of sensual desires must also cease. In the mystery temples of old, all such indulgences were not only severely restricted but *entirely forbidden,* particularly when advance from one grade or degree to its successor became possible. Each rung of the figurative ladder set up between earth and heaven can be mounted only when the continuance of undesirable habits from the past has ceased.

These and other self-purgings of bedulling habits from one's preceding ways of life have as their motives self-purification. This must become progressive until the whole of the mortal man—body, emotions, and formal thought—has become, to use a metaphorical phrase, "whiter than snow." These provisions are only minimal for the reasonably intelligent seeker for that power by means of which inner progress may be made, and maximum health bestowed upon mankind.

Regimes of regular meditation, repetition of personal pledges concerning motives and conduct, and the practice of watchfulness, are all inculcated by the Elders of the race and their representatives out in the world. The task of these disciples is to look out for, encourage, and guide those who are experiencing the spiritual awakening and the call of interior idealism. Even so, almost to the very end of the journey, the possibility of delay exists. In earlier periods of racial history when human Egos were less fully evolved, such errors were made and slips and falls did occur. Very tragically from the point of view of both the individual and the race, abandonment of the total enterprise then became possible. Nowadays, as evolution has produced both an increased number of spiritually awakened people and more capable and able mystics, pupils, and initiates, these tendencies and possibilities decrease. In consequence, the dangers of falls, whether temporary or permanent, naturally grow less and less. Not only warnings found in occult literature and uttered personally by teachers, but also a study of world affairs within the historical era, intelligently read, may provide valuable guidance. In addition, the aspirant can observe actual instances of error against which he should constantly be on guard.

To sum up, safeguards from errors consist of the following: watchful self-appraisal; avoidance of undue self-interest; the regular practice of contemplation upon the Divine; Yoga to the end of self-disappearance and conscious mergence with the divine Principle in nature; ever-deepening interest in and growing concern for the well-being and happiness of all others, leading to service on their behalf and to spontaneous acts of kindness; adoption of a cause or many causes designed to promote human welfare, and impersonal—yet ever rational—contribution to the fulfillment of the objects of those movements. All this should ideally be carried out without undue rationalization, but rather from a deepening and sincere love for others, especially those who are suffering. Thus may the aspirant safely tread the ancient pathway that leads to initiation in the Greater Mysteries.

20

Successes and Failures After All

OF COURSE, EVERYONE knows that—except for a very small and secluded group of anchorites—no one can live, move, and take his place in society as a totally separate individual. No one can entirely subsist alone and in a complete state of independence. Every move toward self-preservation of self-existence depends for success on a varying number of other people, laymen and professionals. Interaction occurs at almost every level, from meeting the physical necessity for food, clothing, shelter, to education, medication, and religion. Indeed, interaction is a key word and an unavoidable fact for every human being from the moment of birth. This truth so continuously dominates life that it is taken for granted, causing one to be unaware of it unless deliberately studying social life and experience.

Similarly, a perpetual and far more intimate interrelationship between man and man—between man and every other manifesting being, in fact—exists in the realm of spirit. Material relationship is almost entirely external, but the spiritual relationship is wholly interior. In consequence, no barriers can ever exist—and so can never function as causes of separateness—between the immortal individual and the level of existence in which this abides. Therein, oneness exists and rules completely and without escape. Matter formed into objects introduces dividedness, separation in universes, the spiritual aspect of which, on the other hand, is limitless and barrier-free.

This result is of supreme significance for both the knower or *Gnostic* and for the whole human race.[1] In the measure to

1. *Gnostic* (Gk.) Knower of esoteric wisdom or Gnosis.

which the heart of Truth is penetrated, and the mind —abstract and concrete—becomes truly illumined, so does the "family" of fellow human beings on earth benefit from this attainment by a single person. Indeed, shared illumination has become part of the underlying and even positive motive for continuance in the great quest. It sustains the questing one as he passes through those arid periods, stages of reduced attainment, which every aspirant inevitably experiences.

At first and through the earlier stages of the pursuit, the neophyte is almost entirely unaware of this intimate interrelationship and interaction. Nevertheless, it is unfailingly produced by shared illumination. Naturally, the degree of effect upon others is dependent upon the individual's progress. From the moment a person becomes interiorly awakened, the effects of the awakening and of all that follows are greatly enhanced. Strangely, it is as if quickening of the evolutionary pace and increase in the flow of spiritual power throughout the whole of a person's nature bestow upon him an added dynamism, corresponding to a stepping-up of electrical amperage or voltage. It is but natural that thereafter the spiritually and occultly aroused individuals carry with them wherever they go—and especially in all spiritualizing activities—a particular and increased potency. This may be expressed as power to awaken in others their own inspired ability to teach, to heal, and in some cases to provide that spark which sets others upon the pathway of hastened evolution.

This culminates in a remarkably full sharing with every other person; for no one, no living human being, is wholly outside the range and reach of the state of consciousness of every other. From the lowest criminal to the greatest saint, and throughout all intervening phases of unfoldment, every member of the human family is in contact with all others, so that in varying degrees each one influences every human being. When full adeptship is attained by one individual a quickening thrill is transmitted at the level of the spiritual self throughout all humanity, particularly for those moved toward the monastic or ashramic life.

Although this somewhat forceful affirmation of the close relationship among all is stated in terms of external reaction, actually the process is also interior. This is especially the case when an individual reaches the stage at which the higher mind,

117

with its capacity for abstract thought, becomes a functioning power. Thereafter, the interchange with every other person becomes interior in that the results are experienced as though from within as instinctual tendencies and not only as impulses from without.

Before leaving this subject, a reference may be made to what may perhaps be named the transcendence of time. Although the statement may seem an exaggeration, every person who, of his own interior volition and spiritual motivation, embarks upon the steep upward road becomes an influence affecting all others who will similarly awaken, not only during the present period but onward into the humanly immeasurable future. Thus there exists a time-free or time-transcendening spiritual kinship between all those who have awakened and embarked upon the Path and those who in the future will live lives of self-training, self-discipline, and selfless service. Perhaps this especial kinship between awakened ones and future aspirants may be somewhat likened to the deep love that can exist between a parent and a particular child—father for the firstborn son or mother for lastborn, for example. This relationship does not in any way negate the normal understanding and affection which binds all members of a family, but consists of an intenser interest and more tender love for the recipient of such parental devotion. Exclusiveness is not involved in the experience in the slightest degree, only a natural accentuation of the feeling of unity. Admittedly, the illustration is imperfect, since the spiritual awakening does not depend on personal relationships. However, the special intimacy to which reference is made does exist regardless of period, position, or mutual acquaintanceship. This naturally becomes more evident and far more potent between aspirants and Adepts.

The upward way is indeed very steep, thorny, and rocky, and it is not unnatural that fatigue, injuries, and slips may bring about falls, as earlier described. These not only affect the one who fails temporarily or completely, but render the attempted ascent more difficult for others as well. Just as an infection in the bloodstream can adversely affect the body as a whole, so a spiritual, occult, moral, or physical defection of one individual can have harmful results upon the whole of mankind. The same in lesser degree is true of component nations, tribes, groups, and families. In major or minor degree according to the measure of the favorable or unfavorable personal condition, each human being, as part of the whole, affects the plight of all men. When one person succeeds, the path becomes a little easier for everyone, and the danger of falls is reduced.

Progress may at first appear to be slow. The light of inspiration may become dim and the intensity of the inward fire be subject to fluctuations. These difficulties may on occasion become so apparent, progress seem to be so slow, and even falls occur so unexpectedly that inspiration may be overshadowed by despair—a danger-point. Physical rest, periods of seclusion, and progressive study of the Ageless Wisdom, are among the most helpful remedies for what might be described as the despair syndrome. The degree of spiritual activity—yogic and physical—may be reduced if desired. Those pleasures of life which do not in any way run counter to the ideal of purity may be restfully enjoyed. In any case, *nil desperandum* must be a watchword,[2] especially for those newly awakening and newly responding to the call of the spiritual life.

Those who succumb to temptation and fall below the ideal should retire into silence and especially refrain from any actions or words which could possibly injure fellow aspirants. The newly awakening person, whether young, mature, or old in body, is especially sensitive and vulnerable to the wrongdoing of those who fall. An aspirant should never utter even one word derogatory of the whole splendid undertaking. He should be silent, be still, not only for his own sake but also for that of his fellowmen.

A kind of battle there must be, however. Indeed, warfare is inevitable and may be described as a war between the past and the present, the old and the newly born, between general custom, habit and the like, on the one hand, and the urge to reform, on the other. Although the decision to improve oneself is interiorly born, the change is largely external, relating to the ways of thought, emotion, and conduct hitherto followed. Some of these ways must be gradually outgrown while others must cease altogether. As heretofore stated and even accentuated, the major alteration at all levels is that self, self-will, self-decision, and self-gain must be disenthroned. These must be replaced by the guiding principle of selflessness or that which is best for others. When once the momentous decision is

2. *Nil desperandum.* Do not despair.

finally taken and the battle embarked upon and some successes gained, the very thought of self—and even the word—fades away, to be replaced by the thought of others.

The nature of this interior warfare and the failures or successes of the two "combatants"—the inner and the outer man—need fully to be grasped. Without undue self-centeredness, they should be studied and the issues fully understood. The region of the mind which moves one to action—motives for the most part—may then respond to modifications, leading eventually to complete changes. When once this mental impulse in the right direction has been initiated and assumes an increasing measure of command, victory will be won and the standard erected over the conquered region. The colors and the symbolism emblazoned thereon will be "deepening concern for others, declining concern for self."

21

The World Problem

THE CAUSE OF almost all human destructiveness and sorrow can on full investigation be traced to absence of the knowledge that division is an error and oneness is the fact concerning human life—indeed all life. That which is so palpably real to the five senses and so visibly unchanging represents neither Reality nor Eternity. The phenomena of the physical world are regarded as real and true, and also wrongly conceived as examples of an unchanging Reality. This is part of the great pain-producing error based upon the senses into which mankind has fallen. Since, for man in his normal state of awareness, these deceptive phenomena of nature and life constitute the totality of available experience, the error—or rather the wrong accentuation of values—is but natural.

Reality actually consists of those underlying *causes* of the phenomena which seem to be objectively real. The checkered history of mankind passing through its age of the development of the mind, demonstrates the urgent necessity for mental and spiritual realization. Intellectual riches are incalculably and abundantly present and available. Mankind gathers some few of them and, with exceptions, misuses them for isolated personal and national benefits. The results are disastrous; for the fruits of research become exceedingly harmful, even destructive to the welfare of the race. For example, Dr. Malcolm S. Adeseshiah, UNESCO's Director-General, wrote: "UNESCO cannot go on spending perhaps one million dollars a year on peace-building when $200,000,000 is being devoted every year to building an arsenal of absolute annihilation. . . . When will we learn that life is all of a piece, a vast, mysterious entanglement of species, that the earth is the home of all and what endangers one must have its ultimate effect on all others?"

Admittedly, noble idealism and admirable ideals have led a proportion of humanity to proclaim the welfare of mankind as their sole objective. Their voices are, however, far too few and, in consequence, the murderous majority flout the ideal. They proceed unhesitatingly to act for personal and national gain at whatever cost to others and however harmful the results of their actions under inevadable compensatory law. It is this self-centered and self-seeking conduct, regardless of effects upon others, that is the cause of the war-ridden, disease-ridden condition of the human race during the period referred to—the miscalled intellectual Age.

All this was foreseen and mankind forewarned by those spiritually illumined superhuman Visitors who have appeared on earth during the historical era. Long ago—even though the fact cannot be proved—they cautioned those who would listen to them and who would read their teachings, warning against the wilderness condition toward which the human race was heading and into which it would enter unless the guidance given was hearkened to and applied to life.

One most serious obstruction to the reception by mankind of the ideal of unity might be described as a deeply seated conviction that man has but one body and one life to live here on earth. Therefore, it is thought he had better make the most of it in terms of worldly success, emotional self-gratification, and security based upon physical means and supplies. However, physical security is not attainable by physical means only, as the tragic war-ridden history of the world exemplifies. The truth is that bodily, domestic, national, and interracial security —implying freedom from danger—is not achievable by sole dependence upon mental and material means. Human beings also have superphysical bodies in which the inherent divine power and Presence are incarnated. So long as this subtle and invisible part of human nature is ignored—despite the teachings of divine sages—so long will men be subject to a continuing physical menace resulting in insecurity and the prevailing fear thereof. Thus, fear reigns in the hearts and minds of mankind, from the humblest dweller in hut and tent to those elected or inheriting responsibility for the security of individuals and nations. This fear—amounting at times and on certain occasions of stress to hopelessness—must ever continue to threaten the happiness and peacefulness of human life so long as that life is regarded as physical alone. Such a belief results in human life being exclusively founded upon and lived in accordance with mental and material activity. The life-story of humanity demonstrates that indeed such a mode of life cannot assure safety or even the continuance of existence. Individual crimes and the criminals who commit them; groups and classes striving for their own welfare to the detriment of less powerful groups; not unnatural determination by the leaders of nations to achieve maximum security and benefits—these have throughout the ages been responsible for bloodshed, war, and death as continuing characteristics of human life upon the planet. Indeed, the nations are afraid of each other, and from this fear arises both the necessity for and the determination to be self-protective and therefore greatly concerned with self-gain. This modifies and, one is tempted to say, almost justifies national and personal selfishness, though in reality it is a form of fear.

Humanity is in these days and in this present age passing through a difficult and dangerous epoch which may perhaps best be described as *conflict*. In almost every area of human activity, opposing interests—national, communal, personal—wage war against each other. Harmonious and cooperative interrelationships between people and nations can be achieved only after many disappointments and failures. They are conceived, molded, and rendered final only with grave difficulty. Allies may almost at any moment find themselves at enmity in both the commercial and the military senses. Erstwhile enemies, in their turn, have found themselves almost drifting into collaboration.

These uncertainties in national and international relationships are indeed gravely dangerous. Even the world, the national, and the group movements toward human togetherness and humaneness—from the United Nations and all its agencies to humanitarian endeavors—find the effectiveness of their efforts to increase human and animal welfare greatly reduced by personal interests acting in contrary directions. The world organization—founded with such high idealism and apparently offering such very great hope for peace, cooperativeness, and collaboration between the nations of the world—fails to fulfill the original ideals. This is because national interests intervene between world aspirations for peace

123

and its actual establishment as an operative procedure on this planet. The leaders of certain nations—happily not all—are unwilling or unable to provide that international collaboration which would to some extent reduce the fulfillment of communal and political interests. UNO should be a center and an example of readiness of each nation to reduce demands reasonably in the cause of world peace and world welfare. Yet it can itself almost be described as a battleground. Involvement in the advancement of political and ideological motivations is so deeply seated in certain people that their representatives at the world body are prohibited from the surrender of any gains for the sake of the welfare of other races. Racial, national, and personal interests overrule readiness to make some surrenders for the sake of the peoples of the world, particularly those close to national borders and of differing ideologies. Otherwise expressed, humanity is at war against itself.

The consequences are all too apparent. Below the surface of human selfishness and determination to put self-gain before all else, there festers a decline in morality. The moral decay behind the triumph of selfishness over selflessness, or ruthless determination to achieve national and personal gain at whatever cost to others, threatens the greatly-to-be desired human idealism, by which alone these problems could and must be solved.

Gurus from the East and scientific investigators from both East and West propound and deliver warnings, point to pathways to safety, and appeal to mankind to forsake its self-destructive ways. While these usefully differ, they naturally fall into two categories—personal and general. The personal approach stresses that the causes and therefore the cures of the dilemma of mankind are interior and largely concern motives for living. The general approach is organizational, stressing the necessity for unity of action in planning and carrying out world projects for the safety and continued existence of humanity. This book refers largely to the former of these two approaches, accentuating the existence *within* man of the causes of so many of his difficulties.

Man continues to be voraciously selfish and, in consequence, indifferent to the sufferings forced upon others by the gratification of his own desires. As the fault lies within man himself, so also must lie the source of danger. The solution—coming from the East—is in the direction of self-spiritualization. Happiness and peace of heart and mind are wholly dependent upon a recognition of the deeper, more interior, and far more powerful *spiritual* aspect and potency with which every human being is endowed. The solution, therefore, of the problems of both racial and personal insecurity consists of a recognition of the threefold nature of man, spiritual, intellectual, and physical, and of their continuing interrelationships.

Man must increasingly change from being intellectually oriented, selfish, and all-too-often cruel, to being guided and motivated spiritually, more and more deeply realizing both unity among all beings and the brotherhood of man. If regarded solely by the mind, the human race exhibits a great diversity; seen by intuitive perception and implicit insight, these differences are found to be largely limited to the surface of both nature and man. Below the surface can be discerned an underlying bond which holds together, in unbreakable unity, all human beings—indeed, all that exists. The physical eye cannot perceive this. The human mind, absorbed with logic based on appearances alone, is also blinded by the divergencies which nature displays and the richness of variety exhibited in man. Spiritual insight alone can reveal the truth that beneath all differences there lies concealed the unalterable fact of oneness. The treasures in the spiritually envisioned cave of Ali Baba do not consist of the many precious metals and stones, whether in their natural state or as built into ornaments, but of the one unchanging diamond Truth—a single existence, one and the same, unalterably identical whether within each individual human being or in nature's substances and forms.

A change is now occurring, and a very radical one. Nature herself—and so human nature and the human mind—is undergoing evolutionary developments in both thought and interrelationships. To use terms from an older age, the "draw bridge" normally raised between the castle of the intuitive mind and the logically active formal mind is being lowered. The moat which hitherto mankind has been unable to span —save for the minority—is being crossed or bridged by increasing numbers of people. All movements, international, national, and personal, for the establishment of a harmonious and unifying relationship between nations and their citizens, are indications of this progress. The League of Nations and its departments, the United Nations Organization and its agencies, and the numerous, if sometimes seemingly eccentric,

125

movements toward better human relationships, are all examples—proofs, in fact—of this interior change which gradually but irresistably is taking place within mankind and especially within his mind.

For example, the Preamble to the United Nations Charter expresses something of this ideal in the common aims of all the peoples whose governments joined together to form the world body: We the people of the United Nations determined

> TO SAVE succeeding generations from the scourge of war, which twice in our lifetime has brought untold sorrow to mankind, and
> TO REAFFIRM faith in fundamental rights, in the dignity and worth of the human person, in the equal rights of men and women and of nations large and small, and
> TO ESTABLISH conditions under which justice and respect for the obligations arising from treaties and other sources of international law can be maintained, and
> TO PROMOTE social progress and better standards of life in larger freedom,
> And for these ends
> TO PRACTICE tolerance and live together in peace with one another as good neighbors, and
> TO UNITE our strength to maintain international peace and security, and
> TO ENSURE, by the acceptance of principles and the institution of methods, that armed force shall not be used, save in the common interest, and
> TO EMPLOY international machinery for the promotion of the economic and social advancement of all peoples.

UNESCO, the United Nations Educational, Scientific, and Cultural Organization, proclaims three main functions: encouraging *international intellectual cooperation; operational assistance to Member States; and promotion of peace, human rights, and mutual understanding among peoples.* "Since wars begin in the minds of men," states a part of the UNESCO Constitution, "it is in the minds of men that the defences of peace must be constructed."

The Principles of the Red Cross include:

1. *Humanity.* Having its origin in the desire to bring help to

the wounded on the battlefield without discrimination, the Red Cross both nationally and internationally strives to prevent and to relieve the sufferings of men in all circumstances. It aims to protect life and health and to provoke respect for the human person. It works in favor of mutual comprehension, friendship, cooperation, and a lasting peace among all peoples.

2. *Impartiality.* It makes no distinction of nationality, race, religion, social class, or political affiliation. It endeavors only to help the individual according to his suffering and to aid the most needy first of all.

3. *Neutrality.* In order to keep the confidence of all, it refrains from taking part in hostilities, and at all times it refuses to become involved in controversies of a political, racial, religious, and philosophic nature.

4. *Independence.* The Red Cross is independent. Though the auxiliaries of the public powers in their humanitarian activities are subject to the laws which govern their respective countries, the national societies ought to maintain an autonomy which will allow them to act always according to the principles of the Red Cross.

5. *Voluntary character.* The Red Cross is an institution for voluntary disinterested aid.

6. *Unity.* There may be only one Red Cross society in each country. It must be open to all and extend its humanitarian action to the whole territory.

7. *Universality.* The Red Cross is a universal institution within which all the societies have equal rights and the duty to help one another.

The Girl Guides Association of Australia calls upon its members to make this Promise:

I promise that I will do my best;
To do my duty to God,
To serve the Queen and help
other people, and
To keep the Guide Law.

22

Kindness - Worldwide

WHEN MEASURED IN purely human terms of historical epochs, millenia, centuries, nights and days of Brahma, the reign of universal love is young, and the night of deliberately inflicted pain is still very dark. Nevertheless, the dawn-light, however dimly, is at last beginning to illumine the eastern sky. Humanitarianism, in all its applications to the relationships between man and man, and man and animal, is finding an increasing footing, a position of growing influence, in the world-mind and in some of the activities of modern man. International organizations for the preservation of peace and the harmonization of relationships between nations, and the many movements toward world brotherhood in various domains, indicate modern advances toward the adoption of humaneness. Movements are being formed and put into action for the reduction of motives of sheer self-gain—national and personal. These, together with many movements founded and governed for the purpose of reducing the degree of cruelty and the appeal for abstinence from conduct which is known to be harmful to others, represent the increasing tendency toward spirituality and responsiveness to the interior ministrations carried out by Adepts in retreat and their dedicated agents out in the world.

Unhappily, while increasing numbers are thus dedicated in both thought and deed, their proportion is far too small. In consequence, in the present evolutionary phase, especially where the gratification of human appetites is concerned, they and their efforts become so greatly outnumbered and weakened that cruelty rather than love tends to rule human life. A total list of activities that lead to the continual infliction of pain—up to the extremest agony—by man upon man and animal would present a statement of fact which could only be truthfully described as appalling. Sincerely motivated though some vivisectors undoubtedly are, the agonizing sufferings inflicted upon animals by researchers in their laboratories are indescribable. So far as man is concerned, the miseries called "accidents" are the products of past, present, continuing, and future cruelties to man and to animal. These unavoidably generate suffering which must later be endured. Not only the inflicted suffering itself but the reactions upon the producers of that suffering under the law of cause and effect are immeasurably serious; for under the law, pain deliberately inflicted by a person upon a sentient being, unless modified by intervening conduct, will be received in like degree upon the bodies by those who inflicted the pain. The world of sentient beings groans in pain which ranges from acute agonies from "accidents," and diseases, sometimes beyond the reach of effective pain-killers.

If human suffering is to be reduced and eventually banished from life, then human cruelty as its cause must be reduced and eventually exorcised from human nature and banished increasingly by law.

It is submitted as at least worthy of deep consideration, that the most greatly needed reform is the establishment among mankind of the practice of kindness. The doctrine of karma may well be advanced in support of this idea in some groups, perhaps intellectuals. This admittedly implies an increasingly general acceptance of the idea—fact indeed—of reincarnation; for in the majority of cases effect rarely follows cause closely in the same life so that the relationship can be seen. For the more naturally compassionate people—the "heart-people"—the appeal is less to the reason than to feelings. Restrained descriptions of cruelty rather than reasoned argument, in consequence, will be more likely to reach and increase their own kindliness.

This Law is:
1. A Guide is loyal and can be trusted.
2. A Guide is helpful.
3. A Guide is polite and considerate.
4. A Guide is friendly and a sister to all Guides.

129

5. A Guide is kind to animals and respects all living things.
Australian Boy Scouts Association: Aim and Basis
Aim 1:1.

(1)   The aim of the Association is to develop good citizenship among boys by forming their character—training them in habits of observation, obedience and self-reliance —inculcating loyalty and thoughtfulness for others —teaching them services useful to the public, and handicrafts useful to themselves—promoting their physical, mental and spiritual development.

Basis

(2)   The principles and practice of the Association are founded on the basis of the Scout Promise and the Scout Law. The Association accepts and aims to preserve steadfastly throughout Australia and its territories the principles of Scouting as founded by the late Chief Scout of the World, Lord Baden Powell of Gilwell, and embodied in his book "Scouting for Boys."

In spite of these hopeful signs, all too often mankind, misled by the senses, driven by desire, passion, insatiate craving for possession, and the power and pride which possession seems to bestow, ignores the underlying and inescapable Reality, the Divinity. This Reality is exactly the same in all that exists, and recognition of this relationship of oneness is the only possible way to personal, national, and international health, peace, and therefore happiness.

What, then, is to be done? *Reversal* is the only possible answer—to turn about from personal and material self-seeking and make total world well-being the goal of all governments in both their interrelationships and processes of internal government.

The remarkable and sage-inspired utterance by Abraham Lincoln ". . .that government of the people, by the people, for the people shall not perish from the earth . . ." now needs —especially in this almost inconceivably dangerous nuclear world—to be succeeded by a further message which may be stated in the four words: "for all are one." International a-greements to place a mutually accepted restriction upon the use of nuclear weapons, for example, remain in danger of being disregarded for national and personal benefits. Unless and until the unalterable fact of wholeness, unity of that indwelling spirit—which is the Real in every human being—is accepted, world disaster threatens mankind. Recognition of world-unity must become an absolutely governing principle in all relationships, between human beings, between man and animals and all sentient creatures.

Then there are those who are neither mind-controlled nor heart-controlled, but simply live their lives according to customary habits with little or no thought or feeling. These are perhaps the most difficult to reach. The appeals of reason and compassion may fail to pass through the dense screen of age-old customs—blood sports, for example—for meeting the necessities of physical life for themselves, their families, and human beings in general. Fishermen fish, herdsmen breed and hand over to slaughtermen the products of their labors, while laboratory researchers into the physical causes and possible preventions and cures of disease, consider the infliction of pain upon sentient creatures as completely permissible, even necessary. For such people, and not unnaturally, bodily needs are automatically accepted as outweighing idealism in pursuits of daily life.

Man, whether primitive or advanced, is admittedly a hunter by instinct, born of both necessity for food and the so-called pleasures of the chase. The miscalled sportsman kills for the pleasure of killing and personal supremacy and skill. This continues to hold high place in the gratification of desires and is an evil which is rather to be outgrown than remedied by presentations of the humanitarian ideal. However, it is suggested, hunting for food and hunting for pleasure should each receive carefully stated attack. The commonsense, practicability, and health-preserving habit of vegetarianism very largely does away with the justification of the very wasteful breeding and killing of hordes of animals for food alone. History is, perhaps, the best source of information concerning the pressing need for the reduction of cruelty and its replacement by humaneness. This applies both to the intellectually motivated or the unthinking follower of those racial customs which became established near to the dawn of human life on earth. The reformer is advised to approach the promulgation of the ideal of humanitarianism with these three main types of human beings and their particular forms of cruel conduct in mind; for each may best be reached along the line of temperament and consequent mode of living.

In the present time mankind tends to be trapped in the mire

131

of ugly and unhealthy forms of emotional pleasure and the prison of the self-separating attributes of the mind, but this will not always be so. The human race moves onward and upward, however slowly. Led by its idealists and inspired by those who have attained to adeptship, mankind will one day become illumined by realization of oneness and moved by its expression as love for all other forms of life. While this gradual development—microscopic in some areas—is occurring, it very greatly needs to be hastened, quickened, and more fully expressed in human thought and conduct. Every truly compassionate person and organization with compassion as its central objective must, in consequence, be regarded as high points, mountains to be ascended as the human race, led by its more advanced members, moves on to the fulfillment of its destiny.

The message to the aspirant who would quickly attain and lead his fellow human beings to the heights must therefore reveal the necessity for this quality of utterly selfless, heartfelt affection to be established throughout the whole nature until it becomes the very fiber of the human being. This will, however, be hardly sufficient unless externally expressed in service to his fellowmen and on behalf of the members of the animal kingdom of nature—so barbarously treated by man. This may take the form of membership in movements designed to increase the happiness and welfare of others, particularly those in grave and great need. The growing idealism, deepening compassion and increasing concern on behalf of the divine Life in all sentient forms, naturally find organized and ever greater active expression in daily life, always with discrimination. The would-be disciple thus cannot permit himself or herself to fall below the ideals of a clean life in the largest meaning of those words.

The individual in whom this interior unfoldment has advanced to a still greater degree, and in whom the expression of this quality of compassion has become an urgent demand that will not be denied, may most surely and most rapidly travel along the remainder of the upward way. The essential means are continuous meditation upon the oneness of the life in all forms, and leadership and participation in organized as well as personal endeavors to reduce the present horror-producing cruelty, which unfortunately does characterize the way of life of some human beings and therefore delays the progress to self-spiritualization.

To this end, all Adept ministrations, the ever-positive and ever-productive assistance of the brotherhood of the Adepts, is continuously given to mankind in the worlds of spiritual, intellectual, and purely mental awareness. This aid may be thought of as a current of compassion-evoking influence with which human thought is continuously flooded. A greater number of human collaborators is greatly needed in this extremely important activity. Prayers and prayer-thought evoke powers and tendencies which, when they find entry into the human mind, move its possessor to greatly increased kindness in attitude and action in all relationships. All prayers in all world faiths and in mystical and philosophic communities greatly assist in the fulfillment of the ideal, and are beneficent; particularly when uttered with strongly evocative thought-power. However, praiseworthy as they are, these cannot possibly produce maximum effect unless the worshippers themselves are deeply moved with compassion. Indeed, without this, such prayers could tend to become mere groups of words uttered and responded to without deep and sincere conviction and therefore with greatly reduced effectiveness. Peace on earth is almost entirely dependent upon the presence within the hearts and minds of human beings of the quality and power of compassion. It is urgently necessary that such prayers be offered, not only for the cessation of wars, but also for the awakening, development, and growth in human hearts and minds of the true spirit of natural kindness and divine compassion toward all other beings in the human and the animal kingdoms of nature. Humanitarianism, the ideal of humaneness in all human interrelationships as well as those between men and animals, greatly needs to become the gospel of the new age as far as the application of religious ideals to conduct is concerned; for mankind must become merciful. So great, so serious, so calamitous is cruelty in the world and in the minds and lives of human beings, that an immensely powerful world campaign against it is vitally needed. From their earliest possible years, children in homes and in schools greatly need and could most valuably receive counsel and example from parents, teachers, and other associates directly inculcating tenderness and humaneness toward human beings, animals, and all sentient life. This would build in the spirit of kindness and a natural repulsion toward thoughts and deeds which inflict pain. A crusade for compassion has already been born and is active to some extent. It gravely needs to be inaugurated on a

133

world scale, chiefly in homes and educational institutions where young people establish their attitudes toward life.

Deeply sincere, deeply felt humaneness arising from compassion is one of the most beautiful of human qualities. When present in the aura,[1] it glows within and shines without in a softly gleaming roseate light. The softness of the hue in no sense indicates the slightest degree of weakness. On the contrary, it becomes an increasingly dominant power in the character and conduct in all those within whom it is actively developing.

Ultimately, cruelty will cease, not only for these reasons, but because, to the illumined and spiritually awakened human being, the deliberate infliction of cruelty has become entirely impossible. The development of compassion grants no place whatever to cruelty of any kind in the lives and conduct of mankind. Thus, one part of the Call is, first, personally to eliminate cruelty from one's own life and, second, to appeal with all possible effective methods for all others to do so.

This must, of course, not be carried out with the slightest sense of either self-superiority or self-separation by withdrawal from one's fellowmen. Naturally, discriminative wisdom must always be applied. Not only must the realization of oneness thus be preserved and expressed, but the very motive itself must carefully be examined and, if the word be appropriate, purified from the idea of being kind in order to ensure self-gain under the law of cause and effect. The real kindness results from kindness's sake alone. The truly kind person is so because deliberate unkindness has become unthinkable in motive and impossible in conduct. Indeed, it is axiomatic that the greater the degree of unselfishness in a reformer, the more effective will be his or her humanitarian endeavors.

This brings us to a renewed consideration of the ideal presented in this book, namely, that by the adoption of spiritual idealism and its practice throughout one's life, the speed of human evolution is quickened. In consequence, all that is noble in human nature becomes increasingly apparent and imperative in thoughts, words, and deeds, while agony-causing cruelties diminish and eventually disappear of themselves. The idealist pursues lofty ideals because irresistibly moved from within. Let those who can respond take part in the

1. Aura—Superphysical emanation. See Glossary.

extraordinarily necessary action; for here is work for the benefit of all life upon this planet that is, indeed, most urgently needed.

23

The Disciple - World Ambassador

MODERN OBSERVERS are not lacking who proclaim that humanity would seem to be treading a pathway toward self-destruction—sensually, militarily, and ecologically. If this be true—and support visibly exists for the view—the salvation of the race from this suicidal procedure must depend to a considerable extent, if not entirely, upon spiritually illumined human beings arising and appearing. The life of such completely dedicated occultists may justly be described as an ambassadorship. This office is, of course, not related either to any country or to any particular school of religious thought. Rather is such a disciple a world-agent for world spirituality, a messenger on behalf of the heads of the departments in the Great Brotherhood of the directors of spiritual power, and all those who have attained to the rank of adeptship. These are, indeed, the great ones upon earth, and their unity or "Nationhood" is not that of race or creed. They constitute *one community,* and it is they who, throughout the ages, have kept watch upon humanity. They have especially made available to the idealists of every world period, the knowledge, the protection, and the power that, if rightly received and applied, transforms idealists into practicing occultists. These urgently need both guardianship and guidance as they attempt to follow a mode of life which is almost totally at variance with general and popular ways of living. Indeed, this service by the elders to the younger members of the human race is one expression of the fundamental principle which governs the lives of all those without exception who have themselves discovered the interior light.

The earth is passing through the deepest and therefore

darkest—from the spiritual point of view—phase of the great involutionary and evolutionary journey of the One Life. In consequence, matter—particularly its inertial attribute—is in a position of great power; it overemphasizes materiality in the motives, methods of fulfillment, the modes of life, and the day-by-day waking consciousness of the bodily selves with which the spiritual Monad-Egos of man are associated. However at this time, the earth is emerging from the position of deepest descent of spirit into matter—or involution. In consequence of this emergence, the spirit of man is likewise ascending into a higher level of evolution, following upon the involutionary phase.[1] Therefore, the degradation—ugly and repugnant as it is, overcome and transcended as it must be—is not wholly unnatural, though the deep descent into which it has led certain human beings is unnecessary.

Despite the degree of self-degradation—moral, emotional, and sheerly physical—into which so large a proportion of mankind on earth has sunk, increasing numbers of people are responding to the stirring within them of spiritualizing influences. In an increasing number the inner Self has reached the outer man with idealism, and these have responded in their outer lives, even though with but varying degrees of success. These awakening and awakened ones are not only valuable and praiseworthy, but extremely important for the sake of humanity as a whole. Each one, in degree governed by his or her responsiveness, reduces the depth of the degradation into which fellowmen may descend. They also render far easier response to idealism and its effective expression in daily life for all who are awakening or are on the threshold of that experience. Indeed, this is true for every single idealist upon earth. Because of the degradation around them, but also and far more for their own sakes, these awakening ones are therefore ideally the subjects of the most effective ministrations which their seniors can bestow upon them.

Of these, the newly awakened people are often most difficult to discern. The germ-spot in an egg is relatively small, particularly *before* germination, though thereafter, it dominates the whole process of reproduction. Thus, also, within the seeker for light the germ of idealism ultimately dominates his or her whole life, and the concept of the path-life comes to birth in the mind and heart of the idealist. Heretofore, it may have re-

1. See *The Solar System,* A. E. Powell, T.P.H., London.

mained asleep, as it were. Gradually awakening, it increases the selflessness of the true servant of his fellowmen. It is at this delicate period in the life of an aspirant—and even at a particular moment in time—that the presence and the aid of an intelligently active ambassador of the Lords of Light can be extremely beneficent. The need for such representatives and agents of these Great Ones who will assist them in the ever effective continuance of their beneficent ministrations is clearly apparent. Every spiritual aspirant is therefore granted an immeasurably important opportunity to discover and to help such newly awakening idealists. They also carry a grave responsibility toward all others who are seeking, have found, and are treading what has not inaptly been called "the razor-edged path." Their watchword might be: "Be watchful, be ever on the lookout, ever available, and with wise discrimination ever helpful toward all in whom is shining that interior light that for yourself has become the guiding star."

Wisdom is needed; care must be taken. The character; predominant natural aptitudes or rays; the environmental situation concerning family relationships and responsibilities; even the education and the financial position of a potential recipient of spiritual and occult "germinating" aid—these may all need to be carefully considered. At the same time—and this is where an almost perfect insight and consummate skill are so valuable—the particular manner in which the approach is made becomes all important.

The first indication or sign to be made to a newly awakening seeker for Truth is, in a single word, *interest,* in the fullest and deepest meaning of that word and idea. One thus needs to feel concern for those of one's brethren who are approaching the doorway of the temple of the Mysteries; for they are hoping, however unsurely at first, for true understanding of the meaning and purpose of life. They may also wish to express that concern as helpfulness suited to themselves and other inquirers. All these in their turn—the seekers, the awakening, and the awakened ones—should be helped to discover that they are not alone in their quest and that they have found a friend who will help in the search. In offering such aid, and especially in choosing the method to be employed, knowledge of the seven human temperaments is doubtless the surest guide.[2] The ideas

2. Temperaments—See Chapter 25.

upon this subject suggested earlier in this book may usefully serve in the choice of approach and succession of thoughts that may wisely and at appropriate times be brought to the notice of the person who is judged to be sincerely and truly seeking and likely to follow the guidance given.

The association may, for example, begin by what appears to be almost a chance encounter. If responses so indicate, this meeting may be followed by slight but gradually increasing indications of personal interest and, above all, readiness to give personal help if desired. Books, pamphlets, and magazines may be made available, particularly to those of the third and fifth ray temperaments who are selecting the most suitable means of service. Giving guidance in helping a group or an individual might appeal more especially to those on the second and sixth rays, while the arts may serve as entrance into the minds of those upon the fourth. World affairs and mystical and occult ritual with their corollaries will appeal notably to first and seventh ray people. These suggestions are, however, but broad indications. The utmost care is needed to ensure maximum effectiveness in the approach to a person or a group to whom help is to be offered, however unobtrusively at first.

Another method is needed for those who themselves ask either for guidance in life or in the recovery of good health. Sickness is always a condition of need and therefore one in which wisely offered assistance is likely to be welcomed. Those who have studied health and disease, whether from the point of view of Occult Science or through progress in the medical profession, can follow this approach. Many people, indeed, who might not be in the least susceptible to philosophic guidance while enjoying good health, may prove to be responsive in varying degrees when overtaken by sickness in some form or other. The intuition will nearly always provide guidance, particularly in the early stages of a relationship. In addition both the Master of the would-be helper and the future Master of the recipient are likely to be observant and to render aid. In consequence, the dedicated representative of the Great Brotherhood is hardly likely to make a serious mistake, particularly if all personal claims of superiority and spiritual wisdom are avoided; for such claims might well cause those of certain temperaments either to withdraw or to be lukewarm in response.

The idealist is moved not only from within but is also profoundly disturbed and distressed by the almost total ignorance

139

of mankind concerning the meaning and purpose of human life, and the errors, and so the sufferings, to which that ignorance inevitably leads. The awakened person becomes an ambassador, not only of a Teacher, but of the high ideal of communicating one's own pain-reducing discoveries. At first, the more simple truths are advanced and in the most easily understandable forms. These include: Description of the true or total nature of man, his sevenfold constitution. The processes which are at work in and upon him at every level, namely a "hatching out" of inherent powers. The importance of knowing by direct experience one's true nature as a developing spiritual being which is the real Self. The marked distinction between this inherent Reality or divine Selfhood on the one hand and the vehicles or instruments for its manifestation and growth on the other, or the immortal human Ego and its fourfold, mortal personality. The operation of the law or unalterable process by means of which the evolution of all that exists occurs through cyclic descent into incarnation in matter and withdrawal therefrom, which in man is the process of rebirth. The law under which all human happiness and sufferings are experienced—cause and appropriate effect or karma—which decrees that at every level of density of substance and concerning all beings, every conscious action will inevitably be succeeded by a completely fitting reaction, implying that every experience is decided by preceding conduct.

In consequence of the operation of nature's systematic methods—particularly repeated births and the law of cause and appropriate effect—the cosmos with its component solar systems, planets, and all spiritual beings associated with them may be thought of as a vast, continually productive *egg*. This cosmic egg contains innumerable germ-spots (Monads) or component ova ever ready for germination, ever being germinated or fructified and proceeding to develop. Unfoldment is thus a law of Being.

The ideal reformer teaches the guiding truths that obedience to the law of unfoldment brings happiness, disobedience brings pain. The discovery, full acceptance of, and application to motives and actions of these truths are of first importance to the human race.

Thus, the world of men is open to those who themselves have become illumined by the light of Truth and are seeking ways of sharing that knowledge, especially with those who exhibit signs of being ready to receive it. Such proffered aid will be more readily accepted if it is characterized throughout by a complete absence of the slightest thought or desire for return in any form whatever. While such truths are generally discovered through revelation by the wise, eventually each person will come to know them by direct experience.

In addition, of course, idealistic movements which have firm foundations offer valuable opportunities for ambassadorship, and in some cases it may be well to join and even ultimately to lead them. What might be described as a retiring disposition is very important as is also the obvious absence of the slightest desire to gain, to interfere, or to rule, which is anathema to many people. Thus moved, the spiritually awakened develop capacity as they serve their fellowmen, and at the same time themselves move forward upon the path of swift unfoldment.

Of what then do the activities of those who have carried out such tasks consist? They have risen through the ranks of the Lesser Mysteries, having progressed therein degree by degree and entered the Greater Mysteries, thus joining the true initiates. The major tasks remain the same. The physical evolution of humanity is under the care and direction of a group of Adepts and initiates who by personal temperament are moved toward the fulfillment of this office. The emigrations and immigrations of large groups of people are inspired and directed to the production by blending of a potentially higher, more culturally and spiritually evolved representation of the human race. Indeed, what might perhaps be regarded as a preordained destiny also plays its part in these movements of the peoples of the world, and this, in its turn, is used by the Adepts to further the achievement of an appointed goal. However, actions of, and interactions between, individuals, groups, and nations must be left entirely to the people concerned—karma playing a large part. All people are, of course, free apart from the pressures of their self-instituted karma. In human responses to adept direction, no person or group is ever subjected to inclinations enforced from without or from "above." Human beings—men and women—although in general totally unaware of the existence and operation of such a plan of racial progress, nevertheless may unconsciously play significant parts, as is recorded in history.

The relatively small number (in this age) of those who by admission to the Mysteries have become aware of this Adept-inspired, racial activity, participate whenever and wherever opportunity permits or their Master or a hierophant directs. One form of such proffered assistance is to bring to the notice of newly forming communities the teachings of the Ancient Wisdom and, especially, their many practical applications to human life. In addition, whether teachers or not, these initiated ones out in the world are examples of the idealism which they themselves practice and follow in their own lives, whether silently or verbally.

The message—if it may be so named—of such people to their fellows may perhaps be described as practical application of ideals and religious beliefs to the processes and problems of human nature and human progress. They insist that unless religion works out through daily life, then its proclaimer is something of a fraud, a pretender, and a practitioner of deceit. These ambassadors of the adept Brotherhood themselves practice what they preach, allowing for human weaknesses. Such, briefly described, is the contribution which those who, according to temperament or ray, make to the more physical progress of the human race and particularly new and developing branch races and nations.

24

Withdrawal from the World

A DEEP-SEATED CHANGE in human nature must slowly be brought about in those who tread the path of swift unfoldment. This takes place, not only in one life, but throughout many incarnations. Worldly interests, hitherto legitimate, begin to decline. Philosophic understanding of the many purposes for human existence is achieved by the study of various world philosophies, leanings toward a religious life, and eventually a distaste for any other way of living. These are valuable because they lead—one may almost say force—the person to win escape from the prison of the personal into the freedom of the impersonal attitude toward life. Incarnation after incarnation this inward drive becomes stronger until, along with others, two radical changes develop naturally. These are inwardly an almost complete absorption in philosophic and contemplative thought and interest, and outwardly, an increasing withdrawal from worldly activities. In some cases the whole process of unfoldment takes place interiorly and leads to increasing seclusion. This withdrawal may be spiritually impelled in *ashram*, convent, or monastery, for example. It may be self-educational or scientific, consisting of research into chosen fields and life lived in or near a laboratory of science. Withdrawal is practiced even today by the large numbers of men and women who retire into religious retreat.

Here again, it is of the utmost importance that withdrawal be undertaken with wisdom and due regard for existing responsibilities, and a certain natural attraction toward the ashramic or monastic life. The desire to be alone and at times exclusively in the company of those who are similarly moved becomes dominant. This state can hardly ever be rationalized; for indeed, when regarded in terms of worldly ways of thinking and living, it would hardly seem either reasonable or intelligent. When this stage is reached, and particularly when the individual acquires the faculty of sanely combining both modes of thought, when conversing for example, and is able to live an inner and an outer life together, then circumstances themselves begin to change. In due course, a monastic or ashramic mode of living eventually becomes imperative. Herein, the law of cause and effect plays a decisive role; for freedom to withdraw from the world and the availability of suitable conditions for doing so are by no means accidental. On the contrary, their provision is entirely law-ruled. Idealism selflessly put into practice in former lives, as well as in the present incarnation, constitutes the seeds, the sowing of which produce circumstances suitable for withdrawal. Fortunate indeed are those whose karma permits them to pass freely and openly from a normal way of living into one that to others may seem abnormal and even incomprehensible, particularly as regards chosen companionships.

At this phase in spiritual evolution, assistance always becomes available. A metaphorical door opens and a trustworthy person beckons or verbally invites the aspirant to enter in. Some few, very few indeed, have found themselves to be—or even chosen to be—alone from the time of spiritual awakening to that of attainment. The stylites of the occult history of mankind have been a rarity,[1] one may presume, and rarer still the successes along that lonely road. Nevertheless, the cave of the anchorite has existed and still exists for those who choose to tread the path in solitude. Even those who have thus become awakened gratefully accept the hand of the guide, philosopher, and friend who awaits every sincerely aspiring soul. Hence, the Mystery Tradition on this earth with its external doorways, courts—outer and inner—temples, and their Holy of Holies; for all of these sanctuaries also have their interior representations within the heart and the mind of those "innocent ones" who seek admission thereto.

Even within the secluded confines of a holy Ashram and half unconsciously at first, there may arise within the mind-heart of a disciple desire for supremacy over fellow aspirants. Though

1. Stylite, the saint who sanctified himself by perching on a pillar, (stylos) sixty feet high for thirty-six years of his life. See *The Golden Legend*, Alban Butler.

this must be denied the slightest expression, it is not entirely unnatural, contrary though it is to the accepted ideal of self-lessness. Throughout all preceding lives among fellowmen, care, protection, clothing, and nutrition for oneself of necessity occupied a large place in motives for action and living. Indeed, successful continuance of personal and family life necessitated careful, and even on occasion aggressive, self-interest. Even after karma and personal interest initiate conditions for admission to a sacred Ashram and the company of the disciples of a spiritual teacher, the impulse dies hard. Though appearing to be dead, selfish interest may come to life again, assume its earlier position, and lead to the possible destruction of all the hopes of spiritual development during that particular incarnation. This, doubtless, is the reason why every great teacher and every author of books on an essentially spiritual life accentuate the necessity for guarding against resuscitation of what may have been presumed to have died—namely desire for self-gain.

There may, for example, be tasks to perform, offices to be occupied, positions of responsibility, possibly entailing association with the teacher of a kind exceeding that of other disciples. Temptations may arise to look upon these as evidence of personal regard and even superiority. There is also great danger of using personal position within the Ashram to obtain for others either admissions or benefits for which one is rewarded financially.

Behind these temptations reaching the outer person, there lurks that which has been named "The Dweller on the Threshold," the vice latent within which, for some temperaments, is personal pride. The desire to be regarded as senior; as a specially chosen one; as spiritually and intellectually endowed with powers and faculties not possessed by others; and that peculiar personal sensation which might be named self-satisfaction, remaining from earlier lives—any one of these may cause a downfall and failure of spiritual hopes and aspirations. Such errors can culminate in what must be described as self-expulsion, not only from the chosen ashram, but even from the ashram life itself.

Every neophyte must therefore be on guard against these dangers, external and interior, and be extremely realistic about motives for everything that is done in association with fellow aspirants. Serious though these warnings may seem, there is little need for alarm for those who truly possess and are wholly moved by, purity of heart. This implies that absolute selflessness in which no thought of gain for oneself in any department of life at the cost of another can have the smallest place. This most desirable, indeed essential, state of heart and mind is really less an adopted attitude than a perfectly natural outlook and way of life. It may be regarded less as a forcibly inbuilt characteristic than the result of the evolutionary state of which it is a perfectly normal expression. Nevertheless, it must be deliberately developed and, if somewhat artificially at first, carefully preserved.

At this point, the idea should be advanced that, while exceedingly helpful when fully adopted, such withdrawal is by no means a necessity for the successful living of the spiritual life in obedience to the above-mentioned rules. No one is expected immediately to give himself up to seclusion for spiritual purposes or to a total change of life-habits beyond the apparent dictates of reason. An aspirant is, however, under certain moral obligations that apply very especially to mental attitudes and physical conduct as the great awakening occurs. Nevertheless, nothing is necessary which is truly beyond the capacity of the person who has arrived at this stage. Indeed, evolutionary development, skill, and the interior decision to attain amid submission to the demands of the more worldly life all contribute very positively to spiritual progress. Although surrounded by objects of desire and impelled by necessity to obtain wealth to live and maintain one's dependents, the truly spiritual person is in no sense a slave of the worldly situation in which he is compelled to live. At heart such an idealist becomes increasingly indifferent to riches. He is more deeply interested in the fulfillment of duty solely for duty's sake. While of an increasingly equable temperament, he finds the concepts of acquisition beyond needs, lavishness, ostentation, and self-indulgence, distasteful. In fact, in his heart he has already —and quite naturally—given up all these things, outgrown them indeed.

The wholehearted entry upon a spiritual way of living—in an ashram or in the world—is less and less adopted in response to any appeal from without or distaste for the falsenesses which so often accompany social affairs. Rather it is undertaken because of an interior aspiration to be free from all this and to give oneself up to self-purification, a measure of asceticism, harmlessness toward embodied life, and the devotion of many hours each day to contemplation leading to experience of oneness with God, in the deepest meaning of that word.[2] Thus, increasingly self-impelled, the disciple obeys the unchanging rules, and even amid plenty he may embark upon the pathway of simplicity or wisely applied poverty.

2. God—Supreme, eternal, and indefinable Reality. See Glossary.

25

The Sevenfold Splendor of the Rays

THAT TO WHICH in the Western world the name of *God* is given far transcends all intellectual conceptions of dividedness. On the contrary THAT is, above all, One and One Alone. The contemplating mystic is counseled to conceive and become one with the Supreme Being as an all-including and all-inclusive unity. When, however, the apparently infinitely varied manifestations of that One are seen from without through objectively perceived effects, then a sevenfold division can be discerned. These are the seven rays or divine qualities revealed in *Theosophia,* and they manifest in sevenfold classifications throughout all the kingdoms of nature, including human and superhuman. They appear in seven main types of human beings, each with its outstanding natural attributes and qualities. All these qualities and powers are within every human being to some extent, but in each of the seven main types there is a preponderant tendency. As a general rule, the more advanced the Ego, the more readily discernible in the personality is the primary ray.[1] The chart at the end of this chapter summarizes pertinent information on the rays.

The preponderant qualities of first ray people are will, power, strength, courage, determination, leadership, independence, dignity rising on occasion to majesty, daring, and executive ability. The ideal of the ray is strength, the first ray man greatly appreciating the presence of this quality, indeed tending to judge the value of all conduct and achievement according to the measure of strength employed. He finds

1. See *Seven Human Temperaments,* Geoffrey Hodson.

it difficult to tolerate weakness in any form and tends to despise those who give in. For him God, or the highest good, is the principle of power in all things.

The most natural first ray method of obtaining results is to evoke from within oneself great will power, to become charged with the determination to succeed at all costs, refusing to consider the possibility of defeat. The apotheosis is omnipotence, or becoming consciously one with the divine Will; for as the first ray man ascends the spiritual heights he must renounce the individual for the divine Will. Thus he uses will, not in the sense of strain, but selfless, effortless, frictionless expression of the One Will. Eventually he will achieve dominion over nature and the outer self. The ultimate objective of this ray is to fulfill a high office in the spiritual direction of the life of nations, planets, and solar systems. Each life is therefore a training and a preparation for offices to be held in the future.

The ideal of impersonal universal love founded upon recognition of the unity of life is the special quality of the second ray. When highly evolved, the second ray person is intuitive and aspires to radiate upon the world, without thought of return or reward, wisdom and love which will uplift and inspire all whom he reaches. He also becomes moved to develop to their highest degree as positive powers the spirit of service and the qualities of purity, refinement, gentleness, tenderness, charity, goodwill, benevolence, harmony, and protectiveness. The highest attainment for second ray people is the full realization of unity and its expression in conduct. To extend the range of such realization and expression is their supreme preoccupation. They aspire also successfully to impart wisdom, to illumine others from within.

The principle of conservation, of life-preserving vitalization and universal and human guardianship from all harm, regarded as an attribute of the Second Aspect of the Deity, moves second ray people. The innate accentuation of this preserving Aspect in man produces in the more personal nature a naturally accepted instinct or intuition that Deity is to be conceived as ever-preserving Life and love. In consequence, and especially when self-interest is transcended, the ideal religion becomes quite naturally a mode of service—to guard, to maintain, and to preserve. This applies equally to the form of the Church Service while it remains still useful, and also to the life and pattern functioning within that form. For such people, what might be described as "the soul of things" is regarded as of equal, if not greater, value than the inhabited form. As evolution proceeds, therefore, the indwelling Life becomes ever more deeply realized and indeed worshipped, however informally. God is Life, and the forms of nature are but the tabernacles in which Deity thus conceived is enshrined. To become one with, merged and even lost within the all-pervading, all-ensouling Life Principle of the Universe, becomes the mystical aspiration and spiritual goal for those on the second ray in whom innately the principle of God as life-giving and life-preserving is accentuated.

Third ray people seek, with ever-deepening understanding, to know the Divinity consciously. Among them are the intellectually illumined people on earth in whom the spiritual centers of human existence, Monads, have become their sources of inspiration. God for them, rarely if ever personalized, is that principle of Ideation and divine Conception of which the universe, and so all human beings, are manifestations. God as Idea, God as Thinker, Ideator, conceiving Logos, is the object of completely impersonal worship. Naturally and increasingly they dwell upon the Logos in contemplative thought.[2] The goal is to attain to a state of consciousness and being in which that divine Conceiver is known and its concepts ever more fully comprehended. To know, to understand, and intelligently to apply highly spiritualized Ideas, such is the mountain top that the worshipper of God as Truth, Law, and Knowledge seeks to ascend. The summit glows with sevenfold splendor. The whole peak is alight without and alive within from that Presence. Such contemplators seek ever more deeply to become at one therewith. The drive to discover, unveil, and inwardly know that underlying secret intellectual Principle or Law is experienced even in the early phases of evolution. Those who succeed are the great philosophers that humanity has produced or, as they themselves might say, whom the operation of the all-powerful Law has brought forth.

While the domain or world of science almost inevitably attracts them, they are never content with explanations and expositions that are wholly objective. These may temporarily gratify the mind but will never satisfy the spiritual intelligence within them. From visible demonstration they seek ever to comprehend those unchanging laws and processes of which the visible is but a temporary, and therefore limited, manifes-

2. Logos (Gk.) The divine creative "Word." See Glossary.

tation. Nothing less than this complete comprehension will ever convince or satisfy him or her in whom by evolution the *will to understand* has become the governing power.

For those on the fourth ray, the directive Intelligence which constructs nature's forms according to the divine Idea becomes instinctually and later intuitionally the center of interest. This is especially true for those for whom the perfection of form shares equal importance with the presence of the divine Life dwelling and unfolding therein. God as Artificer is the most natural approach to religion and its reverent expression as a mode of life for those on the fourth ray. God, the divine Conceiver, Architect and Builder through orders of "masons" becomes the object of the most profound and most reverent adoration. As the power of interior discernment, of spiritual understanding, unfolds, form—though still worshipped—no longer conceals Life and no longer holds total interest. Though reverently approached and observed as a manifestation of the divine Intelligence, it becomes increasingly regarded as a chalice filled even to the brim with the wine of divine Life. Further unfoldment—perhaps simultaneously achieved—reveals also the presence of divine Will in obedience to which the whole process of outward manifestation commences and is fulfilled. Thus power, life, form combine as the divine Triad of Will, Wisdom, and Intelligence, the God-principle of which all nature is equally a manifestation.

Mathematically, the triad is the base of the tetrad,[3] the apex of which represents the forever unknowable One Alone. Thus, to fourth ray people, the universe is stamped with, and expressed by, the number *four*. This constitutes a highly philosophical and yet completely practical spiritual foundation of whatever religious form—if any—is adopted. For these temperaments, the rhythmic harmony with which the divine becomes outwardly expressed can be almost as important as Deity itself. Timing, orderly progression, rhythmic beat, and resultant harmony from the inmost to the outermost expression are the essentials for the expression of that supreme Deity as the principle of beauty, whether of God or of man. By its omnipotence, Deity assures this orderly progression and harmoniousness. Man, evolving toward omnipotence, aspires toward and worships these two principles so that they become the very

3. Tetrad (Gk.) A four-sided pyramidal shape especially valued by the Pythagoreans.

151

"heartbeat" of existence. This underlying, ruling harmony and rhythm is expressed as perfect *order*. The products of fourth ray craftsmen—who might be named "worshippers in the temple of beauty"—display a quality of orderliness which become apparent when the works of inspired artists are closely observed. A certain charm is noticeable, born very largely of rhythmic harmoniousness, grace of line and solid forms, and order in which every contributory portion is given its perfectly planned and therefore appropriate place. From whatever side the result is viewed, total harmony between all parts of the whole and with each single part is assured. Genius, whether in one of the arts or in life, is intuitively aware of—almost one with—this ideal and gives expression to it with increasing perfection as evolution proceeds. Beauty, rhythm, and harmony—not necessarily associated with any known, named, or worshipped Divinity—by their very nature and in every thought, word, and deed are the natural religion of such human beings. For them there *must* be attunement. There must be harmonious interchanges expressed in the arts and, ideally, in every action of daily life.

True, the expression and the forms of such manifestation and fulfillment of the ideal may vary. That which for one is harmonious can be discordant for another, such being the extreme variety of human makeup. Nevertheless, although no words can adequately state the ideal, the poet Keats perhaps comes closest in the English language: "Beauty is truth, truth, beauty; that is all ye know on earth, and all ye need to know."[4] In simpler terms and in the fullest meaning of the word, beauty is everything. The God-Self in the worshippers of beauty becomes more fully and perfectly manifest at every level of human action. Their action and its outward form then more perfectly reveal and express the inward ideal of God the Beautiful, giving beauty to mankind. World peace, for such people, means world harmony. Brotherhood signifies a mutual acceptance of the ideal of beauty as the test and standard of every human activity and created condition. Where discordant ugliness is created, allowed to remain, and even to increase, there is crime, sin, wickedness; for such is the "work of the Devil" for the fourth ray person.

The attributes of fifth ray, as well as third ray, include comprehension of principles, processes and laws which under-

4. Keats, *Ode on a Grecian Urn.*

lie the manifestation of the plan and purpose for objective existence. People in whom these two rays find expression display unyielding determination and untiring endeavor to discover Truth itself, and thereafter to dedicate their whole being and life to that which is truthful. The fifth ray man or woman of science notices and appreciates in varying degrees manifested properties. He finds himself becoming highly concentrated upon one approach to life and one purpose for living. This purpose is to *know,* which is associated with the development to the highest degree of his or her faculty to attain knowledge. He must probe behind facts to discover law and the principle on which they rest. As experiment follows experiment, the personal ability to make these three undeniably clear increasingly becomes the driving force of his life as scientist or searcher for fact, law, and principle founded upon acquired and completely incontestable knowledge. In pursuit of this goal he brings the whole of his mental faculty to bear upon inquiry after inquiry and problem after problem. Nature herself is his temple or, perhaps, laboratory, and therein he calls upon all his powers of investigative thought in determined search for firmly established and incontrovertible facts. A further test applied to the production of perceptible phenomena is that it unfailingly *works.* Thus, this branch of the human family must know, and such people must be able unfailingly to demonstrate their knowledge. In consequence, as the human race passes through a mental age, as at present, such people become the dominating influence in the lives of their fellowmen.

A dilemma confronts the fifth ray person for whom the ideal mode of life might be named "perpetual inquiry." This is due to the presence of a barrier or veil, *Paroketh* in Kabbalistic terminology,[5] which consists of a propensity of the human mind. The discovery of logically demonstrable and physically practicable knowledge depends upon the exercise of the capacity for strictly sequential logic. This must lead to and be based upon accurately designed and employed methods and aids, mechanical and otherwise. As a result, the maximum verity concerning three-dimensional nature is attained. Truth itself,

---

5. Kabbalah (Heb.): "An unwritten or oral tradition." The hidden wisdom of the Hebrew Rabbis derived from the secret doctrine of the Hebrew peoples. See *The Hidden Wisdom in the Holy Bible,* Geoffrey Hodson, Vols. II and VI, Appendixes.

however, is nondirectional, nonspatial, has continuous duration, is free of the limitations of time and of solid materiality of any kind. It is unchanging and cannot be altered, manipulated, or in any way subjected to the normal test carried out at a particular time in the scientific laboratory. Truth is time-free. Physical experiments and their results are limited to time.

How then, may ultimate Truth itself be realized? The age-old answer declared by sages who have achieved has unvaryingly been "in stillness," by the complete cessation of all normal, formal, concrete thought processes. Thinking, meaning the combined operation of the mind and the brain, as occurs in exploratory procedures, may figuratively be described as "noisy." Intuitive perception—particularly as concerns the search for ultimate Truth—can function as a customarily used method only after the activities of the mind-brain have ceased. This is the difficulty, this the dilemma facing the scientist.

In the future, the intuition will operate spontaneously, increasingly intruding upon mental processes that seem timeless when the mind is posing the question. The intuition functions when the mind is in a state of quiet wondering, allowing itself unhurriedly to realize the nature of a particular problem to be solved in the future. At such moments the condition of the mind is such that sudden intuitive illumination can bring extended comprehension and a full solution. No mental effort whatever is needed. The natural dilemma caused by conceptual thinking having been solved, the processes of intuitive comprehension or implicit insight reveal the sought-for truth.

Such a high degree of concentration upon a single objective, if carried too far, can limit the development of other human faculties and characteristics, even blinding the scientist to them. One-pointedness is admittedly of value, particularly when applied to the attainment of a desired end, but it can also be severely limiting where other aspects of human nature and other ends or goals are concerned. Humaneness, for example, in both the personal and the organized life of human beings can be relegated to a position of discovering. As in all human development and activity, being an all-rounded person remains as a greatly-to-be-desired ideal. One-pointedness should not be allowed to produce narrowness, whether of the mind and its interests or of the outlook, character, and mode of living in general.

Sixth ray people are the devotees among human beings.

They in their turn have a large position in the human race. The truly monadic characteristic of one-pointed, dedicated devotion to a high ideal—especially the highest of which the personality may be capable at any given time—is of very great importance. It is indeed of the greatest possible moment that this monadic attribute be totally developed and made objective in the personality. Truly, this one-pointedness must become an active expression of the intention of the Monad itself. The sixth ray person, or the devotee thus directed, thus guarded and dedicated, can become one of the most powerful of all servants of the principle of Truth, of fellow human beings, and of members of the animal kingdom. Nothing less—indeed nothing at all—will suffice, will content and satisfy, than absolute single-mindedness in the pursuit of the ideal of conscious self-identification with the Supreme Lord. This One Alone is no mere philosophic abstraction, but a Reality, for unity with which there is no substitute.

While naturally gregarious and expansive, sixth ray people, too, can fall into the error of an excessive and limiting single point of view. This may lead to grave mistakes and become a severely restricting factor in their general evolutionary progress. Then error born of narrowness may take the place of truth as the source of idealism. The recipient would then fail in both devotion itself and devoted ministration.

The mode of procedure by the devotee and the chosen field and method of service will be influenced by the character and qualities of the other six rays. Nevertheless, the shining light of dedication, moved by compassion and expressed in actions to attain practical results, will ever be of immeasurable value to the human race as a whole. Indeed, even the most successful individuals of the six other rays need for their perfection and that of their life-works this marked attribute of selfless devotion.

The seventh ray characteristics are order, princeliness, and true royalty, innate dignity (a source of vulnerability arising from false pride), grace, the selfless exercise of spiritual power, appreciation of splendor and colorfulness in environment and attire, military correctness of movement—all being exclusively directed to the attainment of the goal. This culmination may be immediate or long-term, precisely individual or general. Men and women in whom the influences of the seventh ray are marked and becoming increasingly powerful, are the ritualists

155

of the world. The seventh ray, regarded from the point of view of its expression in motive, thought, feeling, words, and deed, may perhaps be described by the phrase, "All is one and one is all." Every positive attribute of the other six rays will ultimately find combined expression through the work of those born under the beneficent influence of this ray. Power, wisdom, comprehension, beauty, knowledge of fact, deep, well-controlled, and rightly directed devotion will become expressed in conformity with the qualities of the seventh ray. Accentuations will naturally vary according to the nature of the work.

The key which unlocks doorways and gateways—the same key for all rays—is selflessness. This is because self-interest, deepening selfishness, surrender to total self-concern are imprisoning states of consciousness. For people on the second, fourth, and sixth rays, the danger is not very serious because the keynote and chord of their natures is deep interest in the divine Life in all its external forms. The more consciously sentient these forms, the greater will be the concern. Since people on all rays have second, fourth, and sixth rays as part of their makeup to some extent, these threefold interior safeguards exist for all. However, those in whom first, third, fifth, and seventh rays have become predominant need to be more closely on guard against undue interest in self-development and the attainment of selfish power through developed will and knowledge (even of fundamental truths) and of their application to the external worlds. While for second, fourth, and sixth ray people at whatever level, power is welcomed as a means of aiding the fulfillment of the ray ideals, for these rays the same power personally sought, attained, and employed is a danger to be dreaded.

For these—power itself and positions of power; the possession of special knowledge; intellectual superiority; physical favors such as prestige-bestowing offices, constitute very serious temptations. Surrender to these blind the mortal man to the real purposes for human existence and the intimate relationship of oneness which binds all human beings together. For its victims, power thus sought and attained becomes a poison, which when ceaselessly active can induce very serious "diseases." This can lead to death from the point of view of occult progress in that particular life. At first unconsciously, and later perhaps deliberately, the darkened pathway may be entered upon. One of the concomitant dangers is that hypocrisy uses lawlessness as a means of obtaining self-gain, even while preserving a totally deceptive appearance of honest discipleship. Judas Iscariot is a well-drawn example of this error that leads to "suicide," not only bodily but emotionally and mentally as well.[6]

The safeguard for every single pilgrim, whatever his or her ray, who is treading the upward way is selflessness. When self-desire has vanished and only selfless dedication fills the whole field of awareness, then the choice of method is automatically correct. The Adept entirely transcends the limitations of all rays, the definitive and directive tendencies which influence the choice of method whereby a piece of work is to be performed, a duty to be fulfilled. His is slowly occupied with purposes both ultimate and more immediate. So also, must the would-be Adept be moved. His methods become automatically perfect, since karma yoga has long been so practiced as completely to insure its goal which is "skill in action."

---

6. Matt. 27:5.

26

Present-Day Initiation

IF IT SHOULD BE ASKED, as well it may, whether the Mystery Tradition has been continued through the ages since the early dynasties of Egypt, for example, the answer is most definitely in the affirmative. The Wisdom Religion as taught in the Mystery Schools of the past and still taught in those of today (for they are kept alive on this planet by earth's superhuman beings) provides the answer to those who have proven their worthiness to receive it. That worthiness is less an acquired, virtuous condition of mind and mode of life than the result of the evolution of the human soul to a state at which virtue—in the fullest meaning of the word—has become the only possible manner of living.

Although the temples of old have largely fallen into ruins and remained silent and unvisited save by archeologists and tourists, temples of other kinds have continued to exist and valid rites to be performed in them.[1] Even though in both ancient and modern days occult ceremonials have been performed in visible buildings, the real activity with which they were and are involved is far more superphysical than physical.

Among the world's public, semipublic, and private celebrations of the Lesser Mysteries are the sacraments of the Christian faith, which are performed with a considerable degree of ceremony. The seven named sacraments are: Baptism, Confirmation, the Holy Eucharist, Absolution, Holy Unction, Holy Matrimony, Holy Orders up to Consecration. The Holy

1. Valid—established and accepted by the Brotherhood of the Adepts. See *Lecture Notes of the School of the Wisdom,* Geoffrey Hodson, Vol. 1, bk. 16.

Eucharist is regarded by some scholars as a direct remembrance and continuance of certain parts of the rituals of the ancient Mysteries. If this be so, then a direct and very wonderful legacy from the past is bestowed upon mankind every time the Holy Eucharist is celebrated. In olden days in Egypt, Greece, Assyria, and countries of the East and Far East, the original forms of certain ceremonies which are still enacted, were conceived, composed, and directed by Adepts.[2] Perchance, it is to these great ones that St. Paul refers in his words "the just men made perfect."[3] The great and profoundly impressive ceremonials both helped toward and recognized the initiate's progress toward human perfection or—quoting St. Paul, reputed to be himself an initiate—"The measure of the stature of the fullness of Christ."[4] The possibility of adeptic inspiration finds a recognized place in the liturgy of the Liberal Catholic Church, as for example in what is sometimes called "The First Ray Benediction" and named "An Invocation." In this very remarkable prayer, aid is invoked on behalf of all those present who aspire to pass through what in ancient days were known as the successive grades of which the Mysteries were composed.

Freemasonry is regarded as another survival in more modern times of the ancient Mysteries. Other ceremonies are performed in other faiths, particularly those which include the dedication of a person's life—whether in infancy or maturity—to the practice of spiritual ideals. Another example is the *Upanayanam* which is the Hindu ceremony of the investiture with the sacred thread, the initiation which is the "second birth" given by the *Acharya,* and which constitutes the boy a *Dvijah* or twice-born. The word *Upanayana* or *Upanayanam,* means bringing near to the preceptor who initiates the boy by giving him the sacred mantra called *Gayatri* which protects him who chants it. The whole ceremony represents spiritual birth, and all its parts are significant. As spirits are sexless, the boy symbolically becomes sexless, and being such is bound to lead a life of chastity or celibacy. The new garment represents the new body. The girdle is wound round thrice to show that the

2. See *The Priestly Ideal,* Geoffrey Hodson, The St. Alban Press, London, Ojai, Sydney, p. 55.
3. *Heb.* 12:23.
4. *Eph.* 4:13.

boy has to study the three branches of religious teaching—*Samhitas*, the *Brahmanas*, and the *Upanishats*. Also the sacrificial thread consists of three strands knotted together and signifies the various triads which exist in the universe, such as the triple nature of spirit, the triple nature of matter, mind, speech, and body, each again divided into three as regards action; and so on. He who wears the thread should exercise a triple control, over his mind, speech, and body.

". . . The staff, like the triple wand of the *Sannyasi* or mendicant monk, represents the control that a student should exercise over thoughts, words, and actions.

". . . The one who exercises this triple rod in respect to all creatures, controlling desire and anger, attains perfection."[5]

Another example was brought to my notice while staying in Salisbury in Southern Rhodesia. I was informed that there was a Bantu practitioner of the Balsunga tribe who would be willing to demonstrate his skills. He was regarded as a healer of good reputation, and the title of *witch doctor* was not applicable to him. He told me that when he could not readily diagnose an illness he linked himself with the ancestral spirits of the tribe by means of meditations taught at his initiation. These beings, generally referred to as ancestors, then informed him of the nature of the disease and the best method of treatment.

I asked the medicine man to say something about his initiation insofar as reference to it was permissible. He replied that, of course, it was private. I had, however, caught glimpses of it and asked him whether he retreated into the forest with a few specially chosen people, and during the ceremony was he not made to lose consciousness and pass through certain experiences? Admitting that this was true, the medicine man proceeded to describe parts of the rite. The initiatory ceremony, he said, was performed by another medicine man who was assisted by a woman who sang sacred chants during part of it. The final rite, which was highly secret, took place deep in the jungle.

He had commenced his training when he was eleven years old. At that age it was prophesied that he would become a great medicine man and prophet, the ability having been transferred to him from both the medicine man initiate and his own

5. See *An Advanced Text Book of Hindu Religion and Ethics,* issued by The Board of Trustees. Central Hindu College, Benares, pp. 175-179.

grandmother in a special ceremony which was performed before she died. She had become famous chiefly as a rain-maker through the help which she also had received from the ancestral spirits. In answer to a question, he revealed that among these Central African people a woman can become a medicine man by means of the same training received by a man, and some do so.

Asked further about the ceremonies of initiation, he said that a few candidates suffer considerable pain, although others are able to make themselves immune to it. The candidate is first dressed as a medicine man and then seated before the officiants, who thereupon invoke the aid of the ancestral spirits by reciting very ancient formulas. They then successively place their hands upon the head of the candidate in order to convey the initiatory power to him, after which he is presented with a circlet of fur and shell, this constituting part of the insignia of his office. During the ceremony the candidate loses physical consciousness for some two hours, and on waking he possesses the powers of a medicine man and the capacity to serve as a vehicle for the knowledge and influence of the ancestral spirits of his people. These spirits are regarded by them as the highest of beings, and the tradition of communion with them and of magical works performed by their aid is extremely old. The major ceremony of initiation lasts all day and all night, after which the consecrated medicine man is empowered to initiate others who must be of good moral character and "hold all men in respect without exception."

A further very interesting example of the survival of the Ancient Mystery Tradition came to my notice when I accepted an invitation to deliver a course of lectures on Theosophy to a group of artists in Santa Fe, New Mexico, a cultural center close to the Pueblo Indian areas in the Rio Grande Valley where I was allowed intimate glimpses into American Indian life. Over each Pueblo village and tribe there is a kind of priest leader called a *Cacique.* I questioned the local one concerning his early training, and in response he recounted some of the procedures used to select and teach a youth to become a *Cacique.* Part of the training is concerned with the arousing of *Kundalini,*[6] although this may be only from the base of the spine to the solar plexus, so far as I could judge. It appeared to

6. *Kundalini* (Sk.) The Serpent Fire, a psychospiritual force taught of in Hinduism and Theosophy, which in spiritual illumination rises up the spine to the crown of the head.

me that the clairvoyance of the *Cacique* was mostly on the astral and lower mental levels, and mainly confined to the solar plexus chakram.[7] This type of practice was probably a carry-over from the procedures of the old Atlantean race, the members of which were accustomed to use that chakram for clairvoyant purposes, whereas the Aryan occultist is ordered never to use any chakram below the heart because of the dangers associated with the arousing of the lower centers.

These examples demonstrate the continuance throughout long periods, of practices which may legitimately be classified as of the Lesser Mysteries. Whenever their effect includes an interior illumination and the bestowal of supernormal and hitherto unpossessed powers, then the threshold to the Greater Mysteries begins to be crossed. The latter are almost entirely concerned with expansions of consciousness which lead to deepening realization of what might perhaps be named "God-Selfhood." Both comprehension and realization begin to dawn of the interrelationships between the divine *within* man and the Divinity immanent within and transcendent beyond the universe. As the greatly privileged admissions to, and passages through, the degrees or grades in the Greater Mysteries are granted, corresponding increases of comprehension and realization are brought about.

In the Lesser Mysteries of olden days and their modern survivals, interior illumination is "initiated" by means of allegorical ceremonial actions that are proclaimed to be founded upon historical events. Unfortunately, the tendency continues to exist to regard the whole procedure as allegorical alone, the dramatic enactment of a parable, as it were. The accents are placed upon externally visible symbology, bodily preparations, successive regalias, titles and offices during those periods when the temples are "open." Even so, since the Lesser and the Greater Mysteries are very intimately interrelated, flashes and even prolonged spiritual experiences from the Greater may be passed through during the performance of the rites of the Lesser, especially those in which initiations are directly conferred. Consecration of the bread and wine by a fully ordained Priest during the celebration of the Holy Eucharist, and the mystical effects of their administration to members of congregations, are examples of this possibility and of the fact that

7. Chakram (Sk.) One of seven superphysical force centers located within the body.

in essence, the two forms of the Mysteries are at one. These ceremonies may correctly be referred to as initiations, for in those who are able to respond, the beginnings of spiritual understanding and realization are, as it were, initiated within reincarnating Ego, mind and brain.

Throughout all time, millions of people have passed through these preliminary rites in one form or another, from the purely primitive to the highly developed ritual initiations. In certain cases, the ceremonial coronation of sovereigns has the same meaning; for in this—as also in "dubbing"[8]—the Mystery Tradition is preserved. Indeed, in these and other ways—including the sacraments of Baptism, Confirmation when fully ceremonial—the Lesser and the Greater Mysteries have never wholly been closed.

One of the most potent of all actions in spiritual ceremonials such as those mentioned, consists of the touch by the performing official upon parts of the head, whether by sword or, more directly, a part of the hand. At such times a certain degree of germination and resultant development always occurs within the initiate, whether or not realized in consciousness. In the ritual-act when the crown of the head is more especially concentrated upon, the recipient is most greatly blessed, occultly and spiritually awakened, and linked with his own inner Self. The making of the sign of the Cross with the thumb of the right hand on the crown of the head can be similarly effective, particularly when oil which has been ceremonially blessed is applied at the same time. From the Baptism of an infant up to the Crowning of a candidate, as in certain ceremonial actions and orders, the personal nature—particularly the brain-mind—is rendered increasingly responsive to impulses from the reincarnating spiritual Self. In these various ways, the Mysteries termed *ancient* have been perpetuated and maintained in their ceremonial functions, right down through the centuries to modern days. For this benediction—as for so many others visible and invisible—humanity owes the most profound gratitude to the adept hierophants and their fully initiated disciples.

---

8. Dubbing—Ceremony of Knighting.

27

Close to Perfection

IN OLDEN DAYS, passage through the degrees and grades of the Lesser and the Greater Mysteries was granted after quite serious psychological and physical tests. Courage and the ability to conquer fear, simple virtue, and a control of sexuality were included, as also was a certain interior determination to proceed. In later and in present times, however, these tests become almost entirely psychological and moral, though a measure of physical self-mastery is demanded.

Adverse karma is precipitated during certain cycles and incarnations. In consequence, on occasion physical conduct is unpreventably followed quite quickly—immediately in the same life sometimes—by appropriate reactions that normally would have been experienced in a future life. Karma takes on what might be described as a "whip-lash" quality, so speedily do effects follow upon causes. The main issue, however, becomes increasingly a moral one. Furthermore, the demands can be exceedingly subtle, thereby testing the moral fiber of the aspirant through and through, as it were. Such qualities as complete straightforwardness, the refusal to depart from strictly honest and undeviating correctness, must be displayed, there being no room for the opposite in the character of the initiate and would-be Adept. *Arhats*[1] and Adepts do not "play" with truth. Righteousness—in the best meaning of that word—and utter straightforwardness quite naturally become established characteristics. High Initiates such as these must

1. *Arhat* (Pali) "One worthy of divine honors." An initiate of the fourth degree.

themselves be the very incarnation of those qualities. Instead of showing them forth according to the older methods included in the term *chivalry,* they have become embedded, as it were, or are immovably present in the very heart, soul, and nature of the high Adepts.

In modern days and according to standards which have become acceptable in certain matters—diplomacy, politics, and business for example—a certain flexibility is manifest while negotiations are afoot. This dishonesty for the purpose of some possible later benefits to oneself or to others must have no place whatever in the motives, character, and conduct of the Adept-in-the-becoming. These demands should not, however, be regarded as made by officials in the temples of the Mysteries but simply and naturally result from the aspirant's decision and consequent action to move forward in evolution at a deliberately hastened speed.

The Personage-to-be has always been potentially present in the Monad at its own divine level. It must now be "hatched out" from within the reincarnating Ego in the Causal Body —vehicle of the Monad on the plane of the abstract intellect. In egg-production, hatching, and bird-rearing, it is important that the shell provide a complete and safe enclosure. In the present instance the shell is represented by the moral qualities, which bestows upon them grave importance. Should the shell become broken before the embryonic Adept is sufficiently developed to emerge and rightly unfold, then failure or at least greatly delayed development becomes inevitable. Hence the accentuation of morality in all literature and ceremonial of the highest idealism.

This leads to the greatest and most difficult to develop of all such characteristics, namely that of selflessness, which ultimately culminates in the total absence of qualities normally associated with the self. Hence, in all valid expositions on the subject of the path, not only is total unselfishness in motive and conduct understood, but still further the complete absence of any sense whatever of existing as a self-separate individuality is demanded. Unless this is achieved, at least to a certain high degree, then failure is almost certain to occur at some point. Symbolically, the "egg-shell" must prove perfect if the "chick" is successfully to issue forth as the manifestation of the germinal Adept present within the Monad of every human being. Because of this inward Adept-presence, and of its total significance in undertaking hastened evolution, all externals increasingly decline in significance. At the same time, that which is within—which philosophically includes everything—steadily increases in importance until it occupies the complete mental field.

When one is this near to the goal, ministrations benefiting others have long overbalanced their opposites. Therefore, karma automatically plays into the hands of the initiate. Earthly conditions "collaborate" in the fulfillment of spiritual purposes—an available ashram life, for example. Overwhelmingly favorable karma makes possible that which under ordinary circumstances would be entirely impossible. These favors, seemingly granted by Nature herself, contribute to the successful closing of the Monad's career as a human being and carry it into the superhuman kingdom. The advantages include unusually good health for the body throughout most of the last purely human life. This means that, apart from obedience to normal rules, little or no time and energy need be devoted to the maintenance of reasonably good health. In consequence, almost the entire attention and thought-power may be directed toward monadic transition from the human into the superhuman kingdom of nature.

Adept—and therefore quite perfect—aid is freely available, and circumstances almost miraculously contribute to success. Finance and family responsibilities no longer hinder the Arhat as he or she ascends the final stages of the steeply upward pathway to adeptship. On the contrary, rather than obstruct, these conditions quite harmoniously and naturally provide physical as well as superphysical aid. Externals thus being favorable, the almost fully developed Adept begins metaphorically to break the "shell" by "pecking" from within, while every care is provided for from without. Nevertheless, since in terms of evolutionary sequences, the whole procedure is unnatural or racially premature, all possible assistance is necessary. A great light shines out from within the mind of such a one and deepening understanding is born. This leads to freedom from the mental restrictions of time and into states of awareness, which for want of appropriate words, can but be named "eternal." The mental glance no longer strays, even momentarily, and tendencies to withdraw into forms of self-protective isolation no longer arise. These and all other so-called temptations are no longer responded to. Even inclinations to resume associations with others who in former lives were very close and even intimate have no power to deflect the aspirant from the chosen path.

In all things, the consciously initiated one has become first and foremost an occultist.[2] Although still living and active in the physical world, with its visible and separate beings and forms, he or she becomes increasingly aware of the Life Principle of which all forms are temporary and ever-changing embodiments. He thus contacts his fellow human beings from the point of view of their unfolding germinal faculties.[3] All impacts upon them are carefully designed to aid, increase, and speed· up all the evolutionary processes which mysteriously and even magically are occurring within the objective persons, however little they may be aware of the fact.

From his occult seniors and by their aid he learns that he in his turn continually grows. His stature, powers, faculties, and auric emanations increase, as he rapidly ascends the great ladder of life. He in his turn similarly ministers to all those who seek his aid. An individual who is illumined finds groups of others who accept and adopt him as one of themselves. Opportunities to encourage, teach, and heal arise and are successfully responded to. Spiritually and occultly empowered and inspired, he brings back to the right track those who have strayed, teaches those who are seeking knowledge, and becomes a healer of his fellowmen. Such redirection, inspiration, and the restoration of health are all founded upon recognition that the outer physical person is a vehicle for an inner invisible being. Errors, lack of understanding, and bodily incapacities of varying degree are appraised largely with an eye to the inner man and its working relationship with the outer self; for it is largely in that psychological region that so many human difficulties have their source.

The state of consciousness associated with initiation into the Greater Mysteries becomes far more powerful in its interior effects upon others than it had been during the pre-Initiate stage. As earlier described, Initiation, in its various significations thus bestows upon the recipient a very considerable addition of power to affect others, and therefore also greater

2. Occultist—see Glossary.
3. The masculine pronoun is used for convenience alone, there being no sex discrimination in the occult life.

responsibility. Indeed, strange though this may sound, one may say that each of the Great Initiations not only empowers and quickens the evolution of initiates but also *links* the initiated Egos more intimately with the inner Self of all their fellowmen. Thus the newly initiated one will tend to feel a continually deepening sense of unity with others. However, the mystic union may not at first become a fully conscious realization. True, non-initiates also both pass through and proclaim—in poetry, for example—the mystical union, but this is inclined to be irregular, to present itself to the mind and then withdraw. After initiation, awareness of unity becomes increasingly permanent.

Even in the earlier phases of experienced oneness, an interior life is lived. The relatively external and the deeply interior ultimately become blended into a single state of consciousness and being—one mode of existence. It is as if unity with the One Life in all is the well or spring from which the waters of life are drawn, and active expression of deeply compassionate concern is the natural direction in which, under gravity, that water inevitably flows. This inner life—whether interiorly penetrative or outwardly expressed—is lived quite spontaneously, as when water from a fountain descends into the surrounding pool and from there again arises and falls in continuous flow.

While in much earlier periods of human life on this planet—during Atlantean times, for example—this development, being so to say very abnormal, was more difficult; time required for the closing phases was longer, and anything like immediate success was much less to be expected. Since then, the human race has marched onward along its evolutionary road. Gradually success became more facile and less threatened by failure or delay. Today and in the future the major change is proving to be an increase in the number of spiritually awakening Ego-personalities. These seek escape from the imprisoning past and present and deliberately hastened attainment of that true freedom which can be experienced only when the stature of an Adept has been achieved. The past thus assists them through favorable karma, the future beckons, and the present may see the emergence of a "new" inhabitant of the earth—a self initiated, perfected human being.

28

The Great Initiations

WHILE MAN IS passing through the present stage of human evolution, inward knowing, elevation, and expansion of awareness are somewhat unnatural and, therefore, mysterious to him. Entry into this state prematurely is not without its dangers. Acquiring intellectual knowledge of the existence of "life-power" as an all-pervasive Presence that transcends familiar limitations of forms followed by realization of identity with that "life-power" involves potential danger. Normal concepts and habitual experiences based upon distinctions of many kinds including enclosed, separated objects, are not perceived, do not exist indeed, as far as this ever-active Principle is concerned. Nothing is ever actually hidden from any human being. The possibility of mystical experiences of various degrees of depth and penetration exists for everyone. Indeed, illumination cannot be withheld since it is but knowledge of the truth concerning universal and human existence—namely, that separateness is a delusion and wholeness is the reality. Nevertheless, the effect of such discovery upon an unprepared mind and a peculiarly sensitive and spiritually responsive brain can be—has indeed proven to be—very upsetting, to say the least. Description of the mystical experience consists of words alone, though *in actu* no words can do more than draw attention to and describe it. The interior knowledge itself is entered into in progressive degrees of depth, and it is *this* which is and will ever remain the true fruitage of initiation into the Mysteries.

The Lesser Mysteries are reflections of the Greater Mysteries enacted in enveiled and symbolical forms, which nevertheless, contain revelations of the mystic truths. The major difference between the Lesser and the Greater Mysteries is that, in the former, the interior revelation and the spiritual regeneration are not produced to the same extent in candidates who participate. Those who passed through the rite of initiation in earlier lives may be exceptions to this rule.

In the ancient Mystery Schools tests of some severity were administered and in order to discover and prove the readiness of the postulant to receive the benediction of the sacred Light. Those tests are reported to have been physical and psychological, and were also applied to improve, strengthen, and temper self-control, determination, and develop insight. He or she who passed through was then received into the Sanctum Sanctorum.

Little, if anything, had been revealed of the mystic rite to follow. In Egypt of old a gigantic statue of the God of the temple or figures of other Deities confronted his astonished gaze. Human officiants in ceremonial raiment were found to be seated at the four points of the compass, each somewhat differently garbed. Behind them, seated round the temple area, were those who had already received the touch of the thyrsus[1] and had been presented with the symbol of eternal Life, the Egyptian tau. These Initiates participated in varying degrees in the deeply impressive ceremonial of initiation.

The candidate knelt within the Holy of Holies. The hierophant addressed him largely to receive assurance that he was physically and intellectually prepared to be inducted into the final Mystery. The candidate was then laid upon the ground by the appropriate officials—perchance even upon a cross. Then, after an invocation to the highest and greatest Being on this earth, the hierophant metaphorically brought down the upraised thyrsus until it touched the crown of the head. The candidate then lost physical awareness or at least so fully transcended it as to silence all "voices" of the body, the senses, and the surrounding world. The soul, then freed from the imprisoning flesh, entered those levels of awareness at which the limitations of time, space and imprisonment in a physical body—a tomb indeed—are transcended. The true "resurrection"—the truth of ever-livingness—was then ex-

1. Thyrsus (Gk.) Rod of power used by the hierophant when conferring initiations. It was charged with high orders of electromagnetic energies in order to convey the hierophantic power and thereby produce the desired results.

perienced, and the deathlessness of the indwelling spirit was known to be a fact. Thus, he who has found the gateway to the temple of the Mysteries, and passed through and entered the Holy of Holies of the temple itself, becomes less aware in and limited to his or her normal bodily nature. He thus consciously exists as a spiritual being for whom the body is only an append-age, as it were. Gradually as the degrees or grades in these Greater Mysteries are passed through, deeper and deeper truths become known. The underlying laws of being and as-cending are less taught than naturally realized as part of the universe and man.

Throughout the ancient rites, the sleeping physical body was very carefully guarded by priests ordained to that office, while on occasion incense and soft chanting both prevented un-timely awakening and gave protection from undesired intru-sions. Deep solemnity characterized the occasion. Then at last the officiant took the somnolent body by the hand, called the initiate by both the earthly and the newly given names with such power that the inward Self, preserving its illuminated state, gradually reassumed the burden of bodily existence.[2]

As the Initiate's eyes reopened, the partially darkened temple with its great and majestic pillars; the seated fellow initiates; the hierophant with assistants standing beside him; the formerly absent sense of solidity and weight—these former states were resumed as conditions of existence. Complete quiet then reigned, granting to the new initiate conditions within a consecrated edifice, surrounded by fellow initiates, in which as full a measure as possible of the interior Light might illumine the mortal man. According to the receptivity of the candidate, that reality was either known immediately or gradually re-vealed itself. Preparatory rites and passage through preceding grades or degrees were all designed to assist in the response in consciousness to the transcendent discovery. The initiate rose, was acknowledged, and presented as an initated member of the mystery rite. In the Greek Mysteries the candidate knelt and pledged irrevocable secrecy of all that had been revealed and had occurred.

Reincarnated Egyptian and Grecian initiates and others from more Eastern parts may even today, with the requisite contemplative insight, know and reexperience these solemn surroundings and events. Although these procedures took

2. The occult name with which the initiated spiritual Self is "christened."

place in ancient days and were carried out in various forms, the interior experience remained ever the same. In due course the rhythms of human life brought to a close the Celebrations of the Egyptian Mysteries. Since those days, in appropriate ceremonials and at suitable levels of consciousness, the same privileges have been granted to those capable of benefiting from them; for the Mysteries are never completely closed and, although no longer objectively apparent to the worldly mind and gaze of succeeding and present generations, the sacred rites continue to be performed even today. In modern days the adeptic hierophants still await those deemed worthy of admission and in unbroken continuance still receive and initiate them. In certain remote places on earth, hidden from prying eyes and protected from intrusion, certain physical buildings provide the conditions of retreat in which precisely the same experiences as of old are passed through by the initiates of more modern days. In addition, during the body's natural sleep, the inner Self is drawn into the presence of hierophants and initiates. Thus, the "newborn one" is received into active membership of that Brotherhood of perfected men and women and Initiates by which in very ancient days, the Mystery Tradition was initiated upon the planet earth.

The real helper in Greek Mysteries is a hierophant of the Mysteries, and his aid consists largely but not entirely of the touch of the thyrsus upon the crown of the candidate's head. One purpose for this act is to bring down power from on high, and another to enlighten the mind of the reverently kneeling neophyte. A third effect of the initiatory rite was and still is to awaken into activity and make available to the brain consciousness, the faculty of the intuitive perception of truth. An enormously stimulating atmic force[3] is brought to bear upon the substance of the brain cells and particularly upon such organs as the pituitary and pineal glands, together with those situated in the mid-brain. These receive a distinctly quickening impulse, increasing the responsiveness of wide-awake, brain consciousness to occultly stimulating forces, ideas, and agencies or intelligences, both planetary and extraplanetary.

Such influences favorably affect not only the physical and etheric matter of the brain, but also the parts of the mechanisms of consciousness which are involved in the transference to the brain of powers, ideas, and occult relationships

3. Atmic, of Atma (Sk.). See Glossary under Atma.

from superphysical and superhuman sources. These, briefly, are the force centers or chakras[4] in the three subtle vehicles—etheric, astral, and mental—the speed of rotation of which is increased by the touch of the thyrsus, as also is their capacity to convey the influences referred to. In consequence, an initiate may arise from the kneeling posture in a spiritually exalted and highly illumined condition. One further result consists of a speeded rate of evolutionary progress.

The intuitive faculty resulting from such experience is of great importance, since by its function wisdom and knowledge of the laws of Being are attained. This knowledge includes cosmogenesis and the nature and activities of the archangelic and angelic intelligences involved in those procedures. Words are doubtless used in order to convey such measure of the Wisdom of the ages as is appropriate to the degree through which the candidate is passing. However, the real and the ideal communications are wordless, being largely, if not entirely, beyond the compass of human language.

Thus, the initiate of the Mystery Schools, whether ancient or modern, is an individual who has metaphorically tapped at the door leading *through* the realm of concrete mentality. He has found this to be opening for him and thereafter passed through into a degree of human development at which mind becomes stilled and yet another voice is heard. This is the voice of Truth herself, both welcoming the newcomer and calling upon him or her to step forward into that temple wherein she is enshrined. The figurative name of the edifice—inscribed over the door—is *Reality.*

The pathway to Truth leads ever more and more deeply within, past and through the limitations of the brain-mind when used as an organ of awareness. The motive-power consists of will-thought—an energy which can by use be developed to become virtually irresistible. If and when a person, selflessly moved from within, finally decides that the goal of existence is directly perceived knowledge, then nothing can prevent its attainment. This Will-thought is what may be named "the kingly power" in man. All people possess it, are indeed endowed with it by nature. In the early stages of human evolution it tends to remain embryonic, but as the inward Self unfolds its deeply inherent capacities, this kingly power awakens into activity and eventually assumes command. It rules not only a

4. Chakras (Sk.). Superphysical force centers. See Glossary.

person's mental empire or thought but gradually his or her whole being. Such a one becomes a kingly person in his or her real nature, a well-ruled woman or man.

The quality of irrevocability has been assigned to this grade in the Greater Mysteries; for having traveled thus far in the search for Light and having received a measure thereof—human limitations, the dread blows of karma and physical death being allowed for—the onward progress toward adeptship is not only decided upon but, in a spiritual and mental sense, possesses the initiate. It is, therefore, irrevocable that the upward way *must* be trodden to its goal of the attainment of the stature of a perfected man or woman. Such initiates are those who have discovered themselves. Simply stated, the experience consists of a vivid expansion of consciousness in which the bodily person, limited to the bondage of time with its procedures of aging and its inevitable decease, has little or no place. The initiate knows that he is a being of light, is ageless, and so immune from the decree of death. He is built of light, living amidst eternal light, untouchable by any worldly necessities, deathless or divinely immortal, and full of joy which will never cease. Such is the reality about himself—and indeed about all mankind—which becomes revealed to the initiate as the great ceremonial proceeds.

At least two among many other benefices are thus conferred upon the whole human race by initiation. One of these consists of the preservation against total disappearance of the Mysteries themselves, together with all the advantages, bodily and spiritual, which they bestow. The other benefice is the maintenance of a pathway from worldly life and human teachers to the occult life and adept Masters for those sufficiently evolved to respond. This also is of immense value, and fortunately for humanity such pupilhood has been accepted and practically applied to life by a continuing succession of disciples.

So will the great work continue until the close of this cycle of human occupation of the earth; for no single individual who has arrived at the initiatory stage—or who stands upon the appropriate rung of the ladder of life—is ever denied the privilege and the tremendous assistance of passing through the Great Initiations, stage by stage and degree by degree, until adeptship is attained.

The way is always open to those who experience the longing for the light of Truth supernal and who are ready to meet the conditions and obey the laws governing the quickening of life's processes—with the sole motive of greater helpfulness in the fulfillment of the evolutionary plan. Let each spiritually and mentally send out the cry for knowledge and affirm uttermost preparedness to surrender self in obedience to nature's laws. That cry, already foreknown, will be heard and answered, always in accordance with karma's decree; for even the Adepts must bow in obedience to this rule. However secretly, the initiate Life will then unfailingly be entered upon; for this is part of the hidden life which—in varying degrees of invisibility—is being lived by some upon the planet Earth.

29

Correspondences Between Man and the Universe

THE STUDENT OF *Theosophia* becomes aware that the planet Earth is by no means alone within the vastness of the universe. "Telegraphic" interconnections with the life-forces and the intelligences in charge of manifestations of the Divine in *all* other parts of the universe are perpetually occurring. All worlds at all levels from densest matter to purest spirit are in perpetual communication with each other. No planet is alone in the cosmos. On the contrary, each has its constantly active interrelationships with other planets, satellites, and signs of the zodiac—imperfectly associated though the stars may appear to be when judged by their spatial positions. When planetary and stellar bodies are referred to in occult literature and teaching, the implications are less with the purely physical planets and stars than with their superphysical counterparts or vehicles and the solar and cosmic intelligences whose kingdoms they are. Continuous, responsive interaction includes outflowing forces and incoming energies. Their transmission and reception are governed by what may be referred to briefly as the mutual frequencies of vibration of forthgoing and incoming interchanges. These occur between solar systems, each with highly evolved Director and coordinated subordinates. They are also functioning—however unconsciously under normal circumstances—between the components of a Universe and individual human beings. Thus viewed, our earth and everything upon it, from the most highly evolved directive Intelligence by whom the functional interchange is known and operated, to human beings, and even to every atom of every plane of nature—all these are intimately linked together.

Though humanity is not ordinarily aware of this linkage, those aspirants who study the teachings that include this knowledge become intellectually aware of it. Gradually, they learn both to understand and even to participate in this vast functioning of nature. When—as is completely possible—they enter into a direct personal relationship with an adept-Master, they then begin to learn, not only the methods by which the interactions take place, but to live in harmony with them. They are taught how to make use of cosmic connections in the fulfillment of the processes of living and the tasks indicated by a Master. Progress through the grades of the Greater Mysteries is accompanied by increasingly conscious awareness of and participation in this interplanetary and interstellar communication. Gradually, the actual parts of the vehicles of human consciousness involved in such communication become known, theoretically at first, and the knowledge becomes increasingly direct and deliberately functional.

The Adept differs from human beings in that he or she is no longer restricted in consciousness to the planetary home. Awareness in and of the superphysical planes by which he himself and his planet are pervaded and surrounded greatly extends the fields of his consciousness. As a result he has learned quite deliberately and with scientific exactitude to contact, respond to, and increasingly collaborate with intelligences that are established at those levels and regions. Indeed, the Adept has so far surpassed the range of normal awareness as to transcend the limitations of the planet upon which he has evolved and achieved adeptship. In other words he has become universalized. This process may be said to begin from the time of admission to the Greater Mysteries, whether as material institutions or as states of consciousness.

Primitive man observed and took an interest in moon, planets, and stars. Developed man becomes an astronomer. The disciple—particularly after successive passages through the grades of the Great Initiations—begins to become increasingly aware of the influences, forces, and intelligences associated with those extraplanetary bodies. This is, indeed, part of the fruits of admission to, and progress within, the system of occult training and advancement that has operated on this planet from time immemorial. Direct occult training under an adept Teacher is an extension of the procedures beyond those carried out in normal educational establishments, however advanced. It might truly be described as progressive extensions of awareness beyond the familiar physical, psychological, and spiritual into wider conditions, phenomena, and powers. Thus, as his occult education proceeds, the disciple becomes increasingly aware of and consciously responsive to his surroundings, including their range in distance, delicacy or refinement of forces, and their wavelengths. Actually, these have always been operating upon and within all members of the human race—indeed upon the life and life functions within all organic forms. The initiate, however, becomes more and more conscious of these interchanges. This last word is used deliberately; for within all organisms reactions occur to the influences that are brought to bear upon them from without.

Some examples of these expansions and interchanges may permissibly be here referred to since some of them have already been revealed.

A SUGGESTED CHART OF CORRESPONDENCES BETWEEN PARTS OF MAN AND THE UNIVERSE

"THE UNIVERSE IS A MAN ON A LARGE SCALE"
CHART TO BE READ VERTICALLY
ALL PARTS OF UNIVERSE AND IN THE SAME VERTICAL COLUMN ARE IN MUTUAL RESONANCE

CLASSIFICATONS   THE CORRESPONDING PARTS OF UNIVERSE AND MAN

Colors of the Spectrum	Red	Orange	Yellow	Green	Blue	Indigo	Violet
Musical Notes	Doh	Ray	Me	Fa	So	La	Te
Metals	Iron	Gold	Quicksilver	Lead	Tin	Copper	Silver
The Syllables of Mantram— *Aum mane padme hum*	Me	Total Mantram	Ma	Pad	Total Mantram	Ni	Aum (Atma) Hum (Physical)
Zodiac Signs	Scorpio Aries	Leo Paramatma	Pisces Virgo Gemini	Capricorn	Sagittarius	Libra Taurus	Aquarius Cancer
Planets	Mars	Sun	Neptune Mercury	Saturn	Jupiter	Venus	Uranus Moon

PARTS OF THE UNIVERSE

Human Principles and Plane	Astral	Prana-Etheric	Buddhi	Manas II	Auric Envelope	Manas I	Atma Etheric and physical
Senses	Taste	Clairvoyance and Intuition	Touch	Sight	General	Hearing	Clairaudience and Smell
Elements (in relation to human principle and sense)	Water	Dormant as yet	Air	Fire	Dormant as yet	Fire	Akasha Earth
Chakrams	Solar Plexus	Spleen	Pineal	Throat Heart	Antahkarana Connecting Bridge	Pituitary	Crown Sacrum
Vital Airs	Samana	Vyana	Ida	Udana	General	Pingala	Apana Prana
Tissues	Fluids	Etheric Double	Fluids	Brain	Skin	Cerebo Spinal	Skeleton
Glands	Epigastric	Spleen	Pineal	Thyroid Thymus	General	Pituitary	Cranial Cocygeal
Embryo	Allantois	Albuminous fluid	Amniotic fluid	Yolk sac	Chorion	Amnion	Embryo
Head Orifice	Left Ear	Right Nostril	Right Eye	Right Ear	Left Nostril	Left Eye	Mouth

Rays and Quality	Devotee Sacrificial love Loyalty Martyrdom (6th Ray)	Source and synthesis of all Logos 7. and Monad	Teacher Wisdom Universal love Philanthropy (2nd Ray)	Scientist Logic Mental keenness and accuracy (5th Ray)	Artist Perception and portrayal of beauty Mediation (4th Ray)	Philosopher Comprehension Adaptability Organizations (3rd Ray)	Leader Ceremonialist Will Magic (1st and 7th Rays)
Jewel	Ruby	All	Sapphire	Topaz	Jasper	Emerald	Diamond Amethyst
Art	Architecture	All	Music	Painting	Opera Synthesis	Literature	Dancing Sculpture (Physical)
Characteristic Magic	Devotion	Not descriptive of a temperament	Raja Yoga	Alchemy	Allurement Charm	Astrology Magnetic forces	Will Ritual Hatha Yoga
Healing Method	Faith	Pranic and Magnetic	Invoke Buddhi	Drugs Surgery Psychosomatics Dianetics	Harmonization	Comprehend Cause, Invoke appropriate aid	Mantras Angels Nature cure Massage Talismans
Symbols	(four-petal symbol)	Seven Rays (star symbol)	(cross symbol)	(five-pointed star symbol)	(double-cross symbol)	(triangle symbol)	1st Ray (swastika symbol) 7th Ray (circle with dot)
Religion	Christianity Islam	Sun Worship	Buddhism	Zoroastrianism Egyptian	Freemasonry Orphic	Chaldean	Hinduism Ceremonial aspects of all religions

Explanations of the correspondences between parts of the man's vehicles and the surrounding and corresponding planes of nature include the idea that these are the abodes of intelligent beings. Highly evolved intelligences—far more so than average man—are the regents of the area in space occupied by material planets or stars. This is somewhat like the air surrounding human beings who live consciously within that air and depend on it for sustenance. This is however but a very partial analogy. A more direct and illustrative simile (of the relationships between man—physical, intellectual and spiritual—and the universe within which he exists) is that of a radio transmitter and receiver. These two are built to operate onto many different wavelengths. Man himself is constituted so as to function both as a transmitter and a receiver. This human "station" functions not only on many wavelengths —each physical organ having its own frequencies, for example—but also at different degrees of density of substance, from dense mineral (especially precious stones and metals) to the most refined and subtle substance of which both the vehicles of man and the universe are built. Thus, from physical to spiritual, from grossest matter to supremely spiritualized substance, man can operate as a transmitting and receiving station on innumerable wavelengths at each of the above levels. It is his Monad-Ego that is transmitter and receiver in terms of consciousness.

Other transmitting and receiving stations also exist including sun, moon, and stellar bodies, with their superphysical counterparts and the intelligent Beings for whom they are centers of activity. The sun may, perhaps, be taken as an illustrative example of this condition operative throughout all nature. The senses of sight and touch, based on organs composed of physical cells, enable man to be aware, however imperfectly, of the physical sun. Man's most delicate, most subtle, most spiritual vehicle or principle of self-expression, known in Sanskrit as atmic, in its turn is in vibrational sympathy or mutual frequencies with the atmic aspect of the visible solar orb, which might be named the spiritual sun. Also each human being is in vibrational sympathy and contact with the sun at each intervening level from purest spirit to densest physical matter. Even at the physical levels of human and solar existence a radio-like superphysical interchange is perceptible. Between the sun and a man a constant interchange continues from the dawn of solar manifestation and the first human incarnation in a physical body. Man and sun are even inter-related at the levels of what are known as the formless or *arupa* worlds—those at which the abstract intelligence, the intuition, and the spiritual will function in those sufficiently developed to make this possible.

At these higher levels the concept of the separated existence of man and sun dwindle to a vanishing point. There, more especially, man and sun exist as intimately coordinated parts of *one unit* which is the thought-spirit-aspect of all nature. In his physical body man knows only the physical sun and its effects upon him and his responses. In his spiritual nature and its vehicles, however, he becomes aware of the truth of the unity between them, more and more fully and deeply as his evolution proceeds. Since this information, when fully understood and made operative, can bestow power upon those receiving it, the deeper implications are revealed only within the assured secrecy of Mystery temples.

Governments establish and maintain representatives —ambassadors or consuls, for example—in those countries with which they are in relationship. So also man's individual nature or set of functioning vehicles contains what might be described as ambassadorial or consular representations of the major so-called heavenly bodies that are physically located externally to him. The whole universe, planetary, stellar, and zodiacal, has its representations within the makeup of man, physical, intellectual, and spiritual.[1] These centers are all appropriately situated in the physical and superphysical bodies at regions where matter is vibrating at the same or harmonious frequencies. The planet Venus, sometimes called the Evening Star, for example, functions or rather transmits and receives on wavelengths in common with those of the frontal brain, especially the pituitary body. This organ consists of the anterior lobe, the pars-intermedia, and the posterior lobe together with the cellular substance composing these. Each of these two lobes contains "ambassadorial" presences for the two corresponding signs of the zodiac, namely Taurus and Libra.

1. This knowledge is part of a science which has begun to be revealed to man in more recent times through the publications of the parent Theosophical Society, Adyar, Madras, India, particularly those which draw upon the writings of H. P. Blavatsky.

The interchanges between areas within man and those regions of space outside him occur by means of archangelic consciousness associated with specific frequencies. However, the vibratory correspondence between man and universe is more vital than material and concerns the one life principle that is all-pervading, even though it vibrates on specific groups of frequencies. The interrelationships between each human being and extraplanetary bodies are far more actions of consciousness than material and are governed by vibrational sympathy, as every Adept knows.

30

The Consciousness of the Initiate

THE CEREMONIES OF the Lesser and the Greater Mysteries of olden days, and their true and valid representations in more modern times, were and still are designed to bring about change in man's thought about himself as a separate individual. As is almost universally affirmed throughout the world's spiritual and philosophical literature, in his inmost Self every human being is intimately related to every other. At that level of his being, no man may truly be described as a separate entity, a distinct identity; for however marked the differences may be at the levels of the mortal man, inwardly the spirit in each one is the same, an essence which is equally shared. Indeed, the same actual, identical Life-Essence is incarnate or embodied in the whole of nature, nothing existing without that Presence being inherently within it as a veritable Reality. The religionist refers to this as the "selfhood of God," the divine Presence, and the God within everything that everywhere exists. The philosopher, thus illumined, perceives and teaches of an abiding, timeless Principle which is unlimited by normal considerations of space and exists as an underlying fundamental throughout all nature. Though almost entirely theoretical at first, this fundamental truth begins to be regarded with interest as soon as the spiritual awakening occurs. As the procedure of self-spiritualization is undertaken and continues, what had hitherto been a theory becomes more and more deeply seen as fact of nature, even a law of life. Eventually, when the truth-seeking path is determinedly and consistently trodden, the fact of spiritual unity with every other human being becomes established as a root principle, as basic verity.

Regular contemplation of it deepens that realization. At the evolutionary stage at which the first of the Great Initiations in the temple of the Greater Mysteries—whether "made with the hands" or not—is about to be conferred, theory and intellectually accepted idea become an actual, known living truth. As is affirmed in mystical writings, this comprehension, or rather full realization, extends to include direct knowledge born of interior illumination. Causal consciousness—meaning awareness at the level at which the reincarnating Ego exists[1]—reveals that the spiritual Self of man, despite its misnomer (Self), is entirely free of the illusory concept of oneself as separate from and different from all others. Quite the contrary. The inner Individuality is even without the capacity to conceive of existence in a state of separation, in the purely human sense, from anything else whatever. The spiritual soul is totally unaware of any idea that in the nature of things there could be differences, divisions, and so separations. All is one and one is all at formless levels of awareness—in Sanskrit, the *Arupa* worlds.[2] An abiding "instinctual" experience of oneness with all, and the continual realization that there are no others than oneself, characterize the state of consciousness in which the human Ego exists. Immortal and eternally continuing being, and an overall universal identity are unthinkingly natural at all levels of awareness "above" that of conceptual thought.

The rite of initiation is designed and performed largely but not entirely in order to deepen the experience of the unity and identity of the one universal spiritual Power and Life in all human beings. When the ceremonial is performed—either at superphysical levels or physically when it includes the freeing of the spiritual Self from the body—the inward Self is initiated into the experience of so deep a submergence into the infinite ocean of planetary and solar Life-Essence, that existence as a separate being vanishes. The initiate is "drowned" or deeply absorbed into the one indivisible ocean of Life.

The more immediate discovery which follows upon passage through the rite of initiation into the Greater Mysteries consists of direct experience of the true nature of man, and so of the initiate himself. Figuratively, he is lifted entirely above that

1. Causal consciousness, see *Lecture Notes of the School of the Wisdom,* Geoffrey Hodson, Vol. 1, Chapter 2, Section 2.
2. *Arupa* (Sk.) "Self-possession," not possession by any other. Ecstatic transcendental consciousness. The highest state of yoga.

which has hitherto been regarded as his normal self, the unenlighted person. Degree by degree the mind of the candidate becomes liberated from the illusion of otherness. Eventually the brain is rendered temporarily inoperative, awareness then being free of all complexities caused by the experience of divisions. The One is all-pervading and without divisions. This is the great discovery that illumines the mind of the successful initiate in the Greater Mysteries. In other words, he disappears as he formally and physically knew himself, the illusion of separateness having been as a tomb from which he arises at the initiatory resurrection.

This so completely transcends all customary experiences and states of consciousness that the center of observance and thinking can be seriously, if only temporarily, disturbed. Such, partly or wholly, is the reason for the enclosure within complete privacy of all the procedures of what is indeed rightly named *The Mysteries*. This privacy includes exclusion from public knowledge, not only of the experience referred to, but also the means whereby the initiate is prepared for, led into, and granted the deeply mystic illumination. So will these and their fruits within human awareness ever remain secret until that future period is entered upon at which oneness with a totally formless, ever-existent Principle gradually becomes normal, as one day it will.

On returning to the body and in consequence becoming aware of the form-imprisoned condition of all life, the center of consciousness could become disturbed, deranged, particularly if the change occurs too abruptly. What might be termed "double-awareness"—in which the mind wanders between the two states—can be the result, and indeed is one of the dangers referred to and against which the newly-initiated one must be guarded. Double-awareness could cause a state which borders on mental confusion. This is one of the reasons for the extreme privacy within which the procedures and fruits of entry into the transcendental state are enclosed.

World conditions change as also do man's state of awareness, brain developments, and nervous sensitivity. In consequence, it may no longer be entirely necessary to perform the full rite of initiation in the presence of the bodily self. This may fall asleep naturally in its own country and the inward Self withdraw from it, thus being free to enter into deeply spiritual states, whether entranced or conscious, whether the body is asleep or awake. The true initiation is received and experienced by the spiritual entity that is the immortal dweller in the physical body during the waking hours. It is the inmost Self in its subtler vehicles of consciousness, particularly that known as the Causal Body, which is most directly involved.

The successive mortal personalities live under the domination of time with its divisions of past, present, and future and its experiences of successive deaths and forgettings and new births without remembrances. No such restrictions, however, bind the state of awareness of the inner reincarnating Self. Therein, forgetting and remembering can have no place, neither can sleep, dream, or rebirth, since life continues in an unbroken realization which is virtually time-free and even timeless.

Thus, as the temple is entered and the door closes fast behind the initiate forevermore, a very strange experience begins. This might be described as knowing without thinking; awareness without looking; existence without space delineations of any kind, the compass, now meaningless, having been left behind. Otherwise expressed, the consciousness of the initiate of the requisite degree is characterized by a state describable as "withinness."

During these periods of deep interior awareness, the external world, including familiar surroundings, disappears; for these phenomena are deduced from the normal sense experience and objective, logical reasoning on the processes of living. These processes are all spatial and temporary, and are now found to have ceased. This idea may be difficult to apprehend at first. The mind within the brain may eventually participate in this awareness without interferences by the demands of passing time and three-dimensional space. Otherwise expressed, brain-awareness becomes ever more blended with spiritual Self-awareness and participates increasingly in its time-free and space-free quality. Such transcendence of the normal attributes of time and space is one of the results produced, the fruits attained, by passage through initiatory rites and also by the successful practice of yoga.

Naturally this is very difficult if not impossible to maintain continuously in the face of the ticking away of seconds, hours, and days and the necessity of obedience to the all-controlling right-hand, left-hand, forward, and backward conditions of space. Needless to say, normal consciousness is resumed when—Samadhi having been brought to a close[3]—the necessities of physical existence must once more be encountered and dealt with. When functioning in the brain, the mind cannot at the same time comprehend and admit ideas of space-free and time-free existence as true. Nevertheless, it is of the utmost importance that the brain-mind become capable of thinking of freedom from time, even though not fully appreciating and experiencing it. Consciousness in the brain greatly needs to become aware of the man beyond the brain and the user thereof; for this inner knowing thereafter illumines, controls, and directs the life of the individual in the physical body. Inwardly, however, at such times and during such experiences as are being described, personal life itself stands still. Then entirely without conscious effort of any kind, this having ceased, the when, why, where, and how of all beings and all things is known. This is in no sense the result of understanding born of illumination through reasoning, but entirely a state of all-knowing without the slightest mental activity of any kind.

Such is the yogic state which might be described as "knowing in stillness." Since this is virtually a contradiction in terms, the attempted description of consciousness within the Holy of Holies is prone to give rise to either rejection or misunderstanding. In reply, one can only say that the solution is available solely to those who have entered into the experience of "still awareness." Indeed, such experience does contravene every idea associated with that conscious existence which is—indeed must be—normal throughout vast periods of time-ruled and place-ruled modes of being. The capacity for still-knowing is referred to for at least two reasons. First, in the future into which humanity is quite rapidly moving, the state described will become normal. Second, for those so moved the experience can begin to be entered into even now in this present time in human evolution. Admittedly, references to such advanced states of wholly interior awareness—the opposite of self-centeredness—have been described earlier. Nevertheless, it is hoped that some repetition may awaken in the reader a response in the form of endeavor to enter into this state at the earliest possible time. This illumined condition of still-awareness may be regarded as one of the reasons for continued references to the more advanced phases of human evolution and the realms of consciousness by which they are accompanied. The effect of entry into this transcendent experience is to awaken from within, as it were, that ardent but purely intuitive determination to bring the future into the present as soon as possible. This very experience, whether called conversion or interior awakening, is important both at the time at which it occurs and, when followed up, of the greatest possible spiritual significance for the future. Hence the cries from great Teachers: "Arise, and awaken to that which you truly are."

When at the close of the ceremony, the hierophant calls the initiate back (backwards, one might almost say) into the physical body, the limitations of the brain-mind partly, but not wholly, close over waking consciousness. The memory remains, however, so that while walking the earth amid earthly phenomena, the initiate neither forgets nor wholly loses the illumined state of everlasting oneness and eternal immortality. In order to preserve this, one particular form of self-training and meditation is of very great, if not greatest, importance for those who have been touched by the thyrsus—whether mystically or during an official temple rite. This is indicated by the word *recollection*, and implies that the custom must become established of remembering regularly mystical experiences and revealed truths. However great the necessities, demands, and interests of the outer worldly life, nothing external must ever again *wholly* absorb the attention. The world with its responsibilities and its attractions must never again be allowed so completely to fill the mind that the interior light and its implications could ever be forgotten. Always at the back of the mind, as it were, there must be "the glow and the shine" of the light that became lit, whether spontaneously during meditation or when passing through a valid initiatory rite. God-recollection, self-recollection, and intuitively realized oneness with all must never be allowed to cease entirely.

Due concern with personal responsibilities, intensity of concentration upon mental or physical work, and even the strain of extreme physical activity must always be accompanied by remembrance of intuitively perceived truths. However far and however deeply into the background of consciousness this knowledge may retreat at certain times, it can be retained by practice—difficult though this may seem to be, and the difficulty is fully acknowledged. For the truly illumined ones, "the light that never was on sea or land" shines of itself in the heart and mind of the dedicated seeker for that Light. On occasion, the interior experience will of itself flood and illumine the consciousness. This does not, need not, prevent giving full attention to whatever tasks in life have to be fulfilled.

What, it may be asked, is the nature of this so-called "Light?" Of course, it resembles no earthly light, if only because it is independent of a localized source, whether sun in the heavens or lamp on earth. This illumination naturally must have its Source, even though not localized, and so unlimited, mysterious though this may seem. Actually, in relation to the physical brain-mind that is irradiated by it, spiritual light has an interior origin and perpetually shines. It is the radiation from the purest spirit-Self of man, the Monad.

Two circumstances, among others, contribute to the human experience of interior enlightenment. One of these is growth into that stature of soul at which mind and brain have become responsive to the indwelling Self. This sensitivity has been earlier described and also methods whereby it may be attained and extended. Reference may again be made to the fact that this responsiveness is more directly achieved by the very regular practice of contemplation of the divine Presence within. Realization may be helped by affirmations of identity with this divine Presence, using a "magical" phrase, "I am THAT, THAT am I." The possibilities of interior illumination and spiritual empowerment attainable by this method are virtually limitless. Anyone who regularly practices the yoga of conscious self-identification with the universal, spiritual Light and with the supreme Lord of Light, and whose daily life is as far as possible harmonized with that aspiration, will not only quicken his own evolution but hasten conscious entry into the illumined state for all mankind. As stated before, this uttermost certitude, founded upon direct knowledge and continuing experience, affects in varying degree every other human traveler over the same waters of life and facing the same obstacles and difficulties. Whether or not physically aware of the encouragement, sustaining support, and interior conviction (as with the majority), each one receives either an instinctual stimulus or an urge, however slight, to press on amid all the doubts and dangers inseparable from karma-ruled existence.

Men and women who have felt and are answering the call to the evolutionary heights, in the degree to which they do so are aided by the attainment of every single member of the race. They are thus lifted up, even though they may be totally unaware of the newly liberated ones or of any individual who

191

has arrived at the goal. This continuing interaction between all human beings is of almost incalculable importance. It may well be made the subject of serious consideration, especially by those who are approaching or have entered upon the path, have found the temple gate, and are figuratively passing through the outer court. For those who have been admitted to the temple, have knelt at the Altar of initiation and received the transforming touch of the mystical thyrsus, relationship with all other fellow human beings is of importance; for when a candidate kneels at the altar to receive initiation, the whole of humanity kneels with him.

This interaction at levels of logical thought, abstract ideation, and pure spirit is, if one may use such a term, electrically instant. As each further step is taken the interchange becomes more intimate and therefore more potent. The whole of humanity advances, however slightly, as each single human being progresses upon that occult and spiritual pathway which leads to the snowcapped summit. This spiritually stimulating interrelationship becomes active from the first moment at which the interior call to the heights is experienced. Hence its incalculably great importance. Up to this present time, every initiate has evolved in advance of the normal evolutionary age for man. He has forced the pace, and the pace has been forced for him by the hierophant. In what might be referred to as the historical era in its largest meaning, he achieves that which will only be normal for the rest of his fellowmen in future Ages when spiritual awareness will have been quite naturally attained.

The evolution of man not only concerns the unfoldment of the spiritual soul, but includes the gradual improvement of the vehicles of thought, feeling, and physical activity. The very atoms of these bodies are undergoing their own development, affecting the vehicles as a whole. When, however, the cosmic, solar, and planetary evolutionary process enters a certain stage or phase, then the necessity for the further repetition of the reincarnating method is outgrown. Unless deliberately accepted for purposes of ministration to his fellowmen and the subhuman kingdoms, the initiate of a particular degree need be reborn no more. In the familiar Buddhist phrase, he is "freed from the wheel of birth and death." Further developments are independent of bodily encasements and he becomes "a walker of the skies,"[4] as the figurative statement affirms. Such is the goal in store for all humanity one day.

4. *Khe-Chara* (Sk.) One of the *Siddhis* or psychospiritual powers attained by advanced yogis.

31

From Human to Adept

BETWEEN THE SO-CALLED man and woman of the world—the ordinary person of any epoch of human on earth—and the spiritually successful human being, a considerable gulf exists. This evolutionary distance and difference between the two is revealed by their character and modes of life and by the degree in which occult and spiritual changes have been produced in them. The man in the street is virtually asleep in this latter sense, save when some crisis evokes heroic and almost superhuman qualities and actions. In the Adept, all the occult forces including Kundalini in its seven levels[1]—have become wholly awakened, aroused, and brought into the fullest possible activity. The normal process and natural developments in these directions have been transcended, and by dedicated living and immense endeavor the standard set for man has been attained. In consequence, comprehension of all underlying principles and of active laws has been achieved. Such illumination culminates in complete and continuous knowledge throughout the initiate's whole nature.

The realization of identity with the indwelling Life renders motives and their expression in action, not only kindly in every respect, but marked by their apotheosis—as Christlike compassion. Every Adept is divinely compassionate. Knowledge of most intimate unity—identity, even—with every other human being results in an associated deep concern for their well-being. The sufferings of all men, women, and children are shared and, in consequence, action is taken to prevent and

1. A sevenfold occult power in the universe and man. See Glossary.

relieve them which, naturally, is more effective than the ministration performed by those at the pre-Adeptic state.

In order to understand, however partially, the significance, experience, and position in nature of an Adept one fact among others needs to be understood. This is that all adverse karma has been balanced out of the relationship with the Life-Principle. In addition, an ever-increasing favorable karma has accrued. In this sense the Adept is a being who is self-freed from enforced adversity by what might be described as "munificent beneficence" toward fellow human beings and all sentient creatures. In consequence, all external circumstances are favorable to the general well-being and the fulfillment of a chosen ideal and way of physical living.

One form or way in which the Adept's extra potency and consequent influence manifests is by inspiring those men and women, proven responsive, who hold, or are likely to hold, positions of leadership in the affairs of mankind. An Adept's service to mankind is far less a chosen way of life than the inevitable and continuing result of the experience of oneness with the Life-Principle in all human beings. The Adepts may thus fittingly be described as embodiments of the will to give aid, which process forms a very large part of their external life.

Adeptic aid is perfectly adapted to the production of maximum effects. Mankind, as head of the hierarchy of not yet perfected evolving beings and forms on this planet, receives the greatest assistance. This adeptic service is always designed and applied in order to reduce as much as possible man's pain-producing conduct, and to increase the speed of unfoldment of the inherent Monadic and Egoic powers.[2] In consequence, the applied assistance is directed far more to those two inner aspects of human living than to the person during physical incarnation where the responsiveness to spiritual influences may be at its minimum.

True, as history records, personal visits in physical forms, however temporarily used, do occur. When surrender to compelling interior Will has become blended with the aspiration to serve as the motive for existence, to save from suffering, and to establish permanently in joy all sentient beings, a supremely great Sage is born into the world of men. A Mahatma,[3] a Christ or Buddha, a Shri Krishna, or other *Avatar* appears in the

2. Limitless evolutionary possibilities and potentialities inherent in the Monad.
3. Mahatma (Sk.) A perfected human being. See Glossary under Adept.

world.[4] Those who are in incarnation at that time and are themselves sufficiently developed to perceive and follow such a manifestation of love-born wisdom and knowledge benefit greatly. Since such Avataric visitations are restricted in time and energy available under natural law, this form of adeptic ministration to mankind follows a cyclic pattern or design. World periods are in consequence characterized by appearances among men of saintly people, scientists, and philosophers who are more highly evolved than is normal for the humanity of their time. Time acts upon the Adept-to-be in a special way that might perhaps be described as "time-free." The future inevitably affects the ever-transient present in all growth processes. Furthermore, when a human being draws nearer to superhumanity, the Adept which he is destined to become increasingly influences his thinking processes. Indeed, the call may also justly be described as the "pull," like that of the magnetic North which draws the compass needle. Increasingly the human being responds to the effect of Monadic and Egoic evolutionary progress with definiteness and decision, until total surrender has been made. The inner Adept-to-be—no longer either embryo or youth but now fully adult—not only calls to the occult heights, but increasingly shapes concepts concerning the processes of living. Thus motives and the conduct arising from them are continually influenced by the Adept-in-the-becoming.

The analogy might almost be applied of a schoolmaster who not only instructs and educates pupils, but by his actual presence and personal character greatly inspires them to become like himself. So, also, the human spiritual soul or reincarnating Monad-Ego not only brings about an awakening—in the spiritual meaning of that word—but exerts an increasingly powerful influence to think, live, and act as much like a perfected person as possible. This interior procedure, which is more natural or spontaneous than directly enforced, takes ever greater hold upon the initiate on the threshold of adeptship as he or she draws nearer to that state. As has been earlier indicated, this is a twofold development. It consists of the products of Monadic unfoldment on the one hand and, on the

4. *Avator* (Sk.)". . . a descent of the manifested Deity . . . into an illusive form of individuality." *The Secret Doctrine*, H. P. Blavatsky, Vol. 3, P. 364. Hermes Trismegistus, Shri Krishna, Zoroaster, Orpheus and the Lord Jesus Christ are examples.

other, of the human being's inevitable manifestations of spiritual power and purpose at physical and superphysical levels.

The response to the Adept which the man or woman is about to become is not at first conscious. As evolutionary time moves on and the adeptic destiny becomes more fully established, the influence becomes more conscious. Thereupon, the theory that the Monad of every human being is predestined to become superhuman ceases to be a postulate. It is now a possibility, however remote, and later to become quite naturally a realized fact. The discrepancy between Adept-in-the-becoming and self-realized Adept declines as the two tend to blend into one. The compass-needle is seen to point directly to the magnetic North of perfected humanity.

Such a person—having arrived or in the process of crossing the threshold between the two states—is of great value to his fellowmen. He now represents an evolutionary certitude. No longer is cosmic, planetary, and human evolution in any doubt or even in question. He is a *knower,* a Gnostic, not only intellectually informed and convinced of evolutionary procedure, but consciously experiencing it. He or she may be likened to a person who has long been occupied with the process of crossing a river or an ocean. Hitherto imbued intellectually with the accepted statement of others, he now knows that the far off and as yet unseen bank or shore really exists, that he has arrived and indeed, his foot is placed upon the gangplank and his hand grasps the rail, put in position, as it were, from the other side. In a phrase, he is now secure. Adverse currents, dangerous storms, and other obstacles, visible or below the surface of the waters of life, have been safely crossed and now are left behind. The possibility of failure, of surrender to the motives and gratifications of the past, no longer exists.

The heroic ones who have attained are free from all temptations to think, to feel, and to act for personal satisfactions, gratifications, and yearnings, as these weaknesses have long ago been outgrown. The quality of endurance has been established within by resistance to, and triumphant overriding of, all dangers and temptations which threatened mind, soul, and heart throughout the more recent incarnations. The innermost Self is completely in charge. The symbolic triple denials by the Peter within and the betrayal by the interior Judas can no longer occur.[5] Such a one is safe at last, even amid the

5. Matt. 26:69; 26:14, 47.

greatest dangers which threaten his unfoldment to adeptship. At this stage all thought of enclosed and separated individuality—*ahamkara*[6]—has been, is, and ever will be seen as a complete delusion. This realization has been achieved by the practice of self-identification with that Life-Principle by both contemplation and deliberate shaping of all mental processes toward conformity with this truth. The Adept has become self-emancipated from the thought of "other" inevitably associated with the illusion of self-separate identity. This illusion has been pierced through and through. The natural and even necessary delusion of I-ness, my, and mine, like the reflection in a mirror, vanished when human thought-processes based on self-existence no longer imprisoned the thinker. During passage through the human kingdom, these false concepts are considered normal and even needful up to this phase in the life of the aspirant. Now he has moved away from the mirror, lives no more amid reflections and has found and realized identity with the non-encased totality of cosmic Life. Once this supreme deliverance has been attained, the condition which was essential during the evolutionary journey through the human kindgom—I-ness—can never again inhibit or imprison adeptic consciousness.

The pronouns *I* and *mine* no longer justly apply to the Adept; for he has transcended the normal meaning attributed to them by humanity. If it were possible even for a moment for a man to be at one in consciousness with such an advanced initiate, he would discover that the named, bodily personal nature of the Adept would have virtually disappeared. True, an Adept who maintains a physical body would answer to a name. Nevertheless, deep within his being no self-separate, reincarnating individuality would be found, for no single, separate, nameable, spiritual Ego remains after the full stature of adeptship has been attained. The Adept may truly be thought of as having disappeared as far as the physically incarnated Mahatma is concerned. Many terms are used to describe this vanishment or complete disappearance of the freed adeptic person, such as *merged, melted, dissolved*. Another expression, though liable to mislead, might be "evaporated." Strangely, even contradictorily, this disappearance leaves within the Adept the memory and the knowledge of the erstwhile per-

---

6. *Ahamkara* (Sk.) Egotism, when thus used. See Glossary.

sonal being, even though all its limitations have been left behind.

Such a condition is, of course, a mystery and must so ever remain, except for those who have passed through the transcendent experience. It is best symbolized and dramatized by physical death, and thus is portrayed as a figurative death in the Lesser Mysteries and their representations throughout the ages down to this present day. To the privileged member of these representations, a symbolic death appears to occur even though the initiate who is said to be slain is not in any way injured. In fact, as the deeply occult and wholly allegorical ceremonial proceeds, the initiate is raised from the tomb or grave.

All the supposed slaughterings of central figures—great heroes or even gods, for example—narrated in world mythology contain this hidden significance. Sometimes there is no actual death in a myth or scripture, as in the instance of Elijah who ascended into heaven in a chariot of fire and the post-resurrection of Jesus who ascended into heaven in clouds of glory. These described ascensions without physical death having first occurred carry the same meaning as if the physical death had actually taken place and the immortal Self had risen free in its astral or subtle body, as in the normal procedures of the life after death.[7]

While in the Adept no individual in the earlier *personal* sense now remains, one might say the Adeptic will is virtually all-powerful within the limits of law. This is not only the product of self-training and evolutionary development, for the personality has become unified with—replaced by—that Mystery which may with reverence be named "the Lord of the Cosmos."[8] Thus, the Adept's power is not in any sense his own; for it is cosmic or universal power that can be focused like light through a burning-glass to a point of intense brilliance. In order to comprehend this inward potency of spiritual Will which the Adept has developed within himself or herself, it is necessary as fully as possible to understand identification with the power, life, and intelligence principles in cosmos, solar system, and man. The Adept may be conceived of as a threefold active, fully conscious manifestation of the triple

7. See *Through the Gateway of Death,* Geoffrey Hodson.
8. The Lord of the Cosmos. The Logos of the cosmos as a whole, meaning all nebulae, galaxies, universes, suns and planets.

Logos of a Solar System. The threefold spiritual Self in an individual is a manifestation of the power, wisdom, and intellectual aspects of the one supreme Reality, the threefold Lord. The attainment of union by man with the triple manifestation of Deity is necessarily a threefold experience as it includes realization of oneness with the trinity of each of the three aspects of the immortal soul of man. These three corresponding expressions of the divine Self in man are the God-power capable of expression as divine Will, *Buddhi,* the spiritually intuitive faculty, and Manas, the deific higher mind.[9] To these three unions must be added a fourth—at-one-ment with that same triplicity inherent within all beings and all things. These are the four unities that are self-existent in man, and by yoga practice may become realized experiences.

The Monad of the Adept continues to unfold to endless heights in the course of his superhuman evolution; for the evolutionary process does not cease at entry into the kingdom of superhumanity any more than elsewhere or at any time-period within the existence of a manifested universe. The Adept, therefore, is an ever-growing, ever-unfolding being of divine or Logoic Power, Wisdom, and Intelligence. This implies power symbolically "to move mountains"; wisdom to exist moment by moment in fully realized unity with the transcendent and indwelling manifested Life of the universe and interrelationships with that Life in every form; intelligence which gives complete comprehension of processes in nature at all levels and therefore of each underlying principle and its expression as a law of life.

Not all those who achieve adeptship retain physical bodies. For purposes of ministration they can use superphysical vestures of consciousness. The choice—particularly as regards the plane of nature or degree of refinement of matter to use—is determined by the contribution to be made. This always concerns the fulfillment of the plan of life for the planet which continues to be the base of operations or the "home" of the Adept. Adeptic power or *Siddhis* enable the Mahatma to materialize a body for his use at any chosen level, including the

---

9. *Atma* (Sk.) Spirit; the highest principle in man. The innermost essence of the individual and the universe. *Buddhi* (Sk.) To fathom a depth. Direct perception. *Manas* (Sk.) The higher mind, the individuality or Ego (spiritual soul).

physical.[10] Such a temporarily formed body would, however, be hypersensitive and its employment limited accordingly.

If a physical body is retained, then its cells have become so highly refined as almost to have evolved beyond the necessities for nutrition by normal human processes. Consciousness has become so universalized that the highly sensitized and responsive body, organs, and cells are self-restoring as if supplied from a universal source of virtually aerial nutriment. Also, need for sleep has become greatly reduced. The extremely heightened bodily sensitivity which accompanies the spiritual attainment of perfected womanhood or manhood increasingly necessitates withdrawal into a seclusion. While the body can be guarded by the exercise of occult protective power, as does occur, the force required can be put to far greater benefit to humanity and other forms of existence. For this reason, Adepts and those who closely approach that evolutionary position have withdrawn into a seclusion wherein discordances find no place. On the contrary, what might be described as every note and chord of physical experience—sound, light, vitality, emotion, and thought—contributes to the complete harmony. A further reason for retirement from the world is the all-important need for privacy which permits the devotion of the whole of their powers and faculties to impersonal and beneficent purposes with assurance of complete freedom from any interruption. The Adept is continuously engaged in work for the world. His life consists of continuous ministration on behalf of the indwelling and evolving Spirit-Essence of the planet and its embodiments in the immense variety of forms. These are among the many reasons why physically incarnate Adepts do not make themselves more available in the world.

In later centuries their number will increase, while the evolutionary time-period required for such attainment will, in its turn, decrease. Gradually, all human beings will become sensitized at the levels referred to and their separations from one another as now, will become less and less necessary. As the number of members of the Adept hierarchy of the planet earth increases, Adept ministration to men and animals will enlarge, extend into wider fields, such benefices will then be more effective in producing the results at which such ministration is aimed, in a word, spiritualized.

10. *Siddhi* (Sk.) An extraordinary power over nature attained by the power of yoga.

Two pathways are open to the self-perfected one, the new entrant into the kingdom of superhumanity. One of these is to withdraw entirely from the objective universe, permitting oneself to be wholly absorbed into the limitless ocean of the ONE LIFE. The cosmos with all its components—including that world upon which perfection was attained—are manifestations of that formless Life. Absorption, disappearance, resumption of the primal state known as Nirvana but imperfectly comprehended, then occurs.[11] On the other pathway, the capacity for objective consciousness is continued and preserved; for it leads, not finally away from, but ever closer to the universe of living beings and nature's forms. Whatever the sacrifice might seem to be, and even may be, the *Nirmanakaya* Adept, even before attainment, chose to remain consciously as part of every living creature and, in fact, of all things in existence.[12] Wholeness, oneness, intimate closeness, and a highly sublimated and nonpersonalized compassion are overmasteringly the cause of the choice—if indeed choice it may be said to be. The decision is so deeply interior that the concept of two choices and two paths is hardly adequate; for the initiate, though still human, knew his or her future as Adept, an inborn decision declared itself. Thereafter, the arisen Master and fellow beings are as one, the materially apparent separateness having become known to be complete illusion. From within, from the very most interior center of existence and consciousness, the fact of oneness evermore proves to be the overriding truth. Love, in the most impersonal meaning of that great word, deepest concern and care for the well-being of all sentient components of cosmos and solar system and with dwellers upon the same planet—these become incarnate in both the individual and personal life. The spiritually glorified Being remains on earth to share in, and when possible to reduce, the trials of subhuman and human beings.

This subject of the pathway followed by those Adepts who remain in contact with objective life, beings, and things is

11. Nirvana (Sk.) Having life extinguished. Conscious absorption in the One Life of the Cosmos, or absolute consciousness (Buddhism).

12. *Nirmanakaya* (Sk.) "Having reached his goal and refused its fruition, he remains on earth, as an Adept; and when he dies, instead of going into Nirvana, he remains in that glorious body he has woven for himself, invisible to uninitiated mankind, to watch over and protect it." *The Voice of the Silence,* H. P. Blavatsky.

introduced and, however partially here considered. It is included for the guidance of all aspirants to spiritual awareness and attainment, to ensure that unmistakably they may hereinafter *know* that throughout the great endeavor, there must be an ever-declining and eventual disappearance of every quality that could be named self-interest. Even as the foot of the neophyte takes its first step toward the gateway of a temple of the Mysteries, even as self-purification and self-illumination begin to be essayed, the hitherto not unnatural thought of self-gain must begin to be dissolved as a charateristic of the would-be initiate into the Lesser and Greater Mysteries.

This reference to and very partial description of the goal of Adeptship is here offered largely as guidance to all who, moved from within, are looking and even moving toward this attainment; for by knowing the goal, if only in terms of an ideal, one may be guided toward it, mentally, emotionally, and physically.

32

Hope for the Future

THE ELDER BROTHERS of the human Race continue faithfully to serve humanity in so many ways thereby give assurance of compassionate and effective care, especially throughout what has proved to be the spiritually darkened periods of human history. Not only then, however, but *always,* this adeptic ministration is continually performed and bestowed. In addition to the *Avatars,* as previously mentioned, Adepts and their disciples appear in the world at times and in places most favorable to the reception and effectiveness of their presence and their teaching. Nevertheless, all these visitations occur under the rule of time and, in consequence, their appearances have beginnings and endings, however gradual. Periods in the history of mankind are found to be marked by relative religious, scientific, and philosophical darknesses, as they are called. In the subjective world, however, spiritual, cultural, and intellectual aid is continuously and without intermission bestowed.

The dual problems of human responsiveness in general and active responses by particular individuals to spiritual and philosophic inspiration naturally play an overriding part in these procedures. While evolutionary progress is hastened thereby, the human tendency to live as a self-interested and nationally concerned person inevitably reduces the degree of favorable reactions. During passage through ages in which the major human development is of the mental vehicle and capacity of man, responses tend to be self-centered and people may be primarily interested in the world of visible, tangible substance—the physical world, in fact. This absorption, while natural, both shuts out spiritualizing influences and consequently reduces their application to physical life. While this condition still obtains, human life on earth is heavily darkened by war and the threat of war, by crimes, and by diseases and sickness. Nevertheless, a light is shining in the darkness, as if a sun were rising, however gradually, in the East.

This glimmering may be designated as progress toward the unification of all mental activities. Philosophical thinking and thought based upon objective observations is becoming blended and will ultimately become unified into a single power which may be called *comprehension.* The organized introduction, or rather reintroduction of Theosophy *(Theosophia, Brahmavidya),* which includes the call to exercise the intuitive mentality, was timed by the great Sages to coincide with and assist this interior development. This is evidenced by the founding and worldwide extension of The Theosophical Society with its promulgation of theosophical principles, the appearance from Eastern countries of spiritual teachers and genuine yogic gurus, bringing the Ancient Wisdom to the attention of mankind.

Indeed, the period was well chosen, not only to stimulate in students the unfoldment of the capacity for abstract thinking, but also in an endeavor to reduce the areas and the intensity of the conflicts of this century, which were clearly foreseen. For many students collaboration with both nature and her perfected men and women has become natural, and these in their turn may become teachers and writers. This development has largely occurred in response to adeptic stimulation of higher mental activity within as large a number as possible of their younger, still human, brothers and sisters.

While it is not the purpose of this book either to discuss or even suggest particular methods of propaganda, nevertheless the expression of some thoughts upon this important subject is virtually unavoidable. In the past hundred years or so since the Theosophical Movement was launched, and even throughout the known historical period—which is very limited in terms of planetary time—the human intellect has been passing through a phase of evolution from entire dependence upon objective phenomena to subjective and intuitive intellection. At present, however, the change is proceeding at a more rapid rate. The so-called bridge between the abstract and the formal areas and functions of the human mind is not only being crossed by increasing numbers of people, but in a few is even disappearing. The effect of this is to bring about quite natural intrusion of intuitively perceived ideas and even knowledge into the more regular and ideally logical functions of the human mind, including physical awareness. In a phrase, man is becoming an intuitive creature.

The problem for the researcher in any field today involves the faculty of allowing this deeply interior power of "knowing" to function at will or demand. The discovery of truth by no means involves the development and use of a capacity that has been unknown and unknowable; for throughout the ages Archimedes-like men and women have exclaimed, "Eureka!" Mystics, philosophers, artists, and those who have totally given themselves to service for the well-being of their fellowmen have all experienced the intrusion into purely mental activities of a revealed wisdom, the revelation of which proved to be far ahead of its time.

The mystics—deeply absorbed in contemplation of the formless, timeless, space-free divine Principle designated Truth—are the real leaders of mankind in this great quest. Nevertheless, legitimate methods of research—meaning painless to all sentient beings and selfless in motive—must and will continue. The call of this period of the present age and of its more immediate successor is for men and women who, with the requisite technique, will probe past worlds and conditions of forms into that formless state wherein Truth ever abides.

This to a large extent is the explanation of the changes which are becoming evident in the attitude of younger people toward living. They find themselves in rebellion against the inequities, injustices, and all-too-frequent criminality characteristic of human conduct—as they see it—especially among the wealthier classes. While this might perhaps be named "the rebellion of youth," the phenomenon has its roots much deeper than mentally observed systems. These roots are embedded in, and are growing out of, a newly awakening level of human consciousness—that from which intuition arises. In consequence, the conduct of those thus moved—notably but not entirely young people—appears to be somewhat illogical. This is because such reasoning pays little or no respect to the achievements of the human race and its highly organized—however faultily planned—method of living and coordination of efforts and systems. This is admittedly imperfect from certain points of view—disparities between "haves" and "have-nots," rich and poor, uneducated and educated, and those of differing color, for example.

The rebels may well be advised to remember that this system with all its faults, particularly its inequities, is itself of relatively recent growth. To break away from it in disgust without endeavoring to produce a workable succssor or even improvement is also a mistake, and in some ways an unjust mistake. The mere flouting of existing methods and restrictions without advancing workable solutions is itself an error that will eventually be outgrown. In truth, both movements—the established system and the "rebellion" of youth—are still young in promoting man's self-civilization. In consequence, they display faults. As the two become merged, however gradually, then the possibility of an almost perfect society, a veritable Utopia indeed, will begin to exist. Sooner or later many individuals and groups must arise for the admittedly necessary and greatly desired changes in human society to be brought about.

The whole problem of human error and its karmic consequences—tragic in the extreme though they have been and continue to be—is both a result and a symptom of immaturity; for the reincarnating spiritual Self of the vast majority of human beings is still immature. Although in itself divine, it is as yet unable to order the conduct of matter-blinded and matter-deafened personalities according to its own idealism. The consequence, to say the very least, is a world history in this epoch containing much that can only be described as filled with horror. Knowledge alone can bring the human race out of its ignorance-born, self-produced misery and calamity.

Happily, nature's evolutionary process has already brought this knowledge to certain men, and at this time is doing so to an increasing number of people. Human history, though darkened, is illumined by the appearance of those perfectd men and women who have run the evolutionary race far ahead of their fellows. With one voice, as the records of history indicate and world scriptures demonstrate, these divine, superhuman Visitors have enunciated among others these two fundamental verities, namely that all life within all forms is One Life and that all deliberate actions produce corresponding reactions. With one voice they teach the oneness of the life in all beings and the inevadable law of cause and effect.

Today, the number of those evolving through the limitations of membership of the human race who have arrived at this knowledge and the understanding which it bestows is steadily increasing. Three results of their evolutionary progress—among many others—are: one, personal conformity to conceived ideals; two, public enunciation of these and associated truths; and, three, as heretofore stated, the founding of movements by nations and groups of individuals designed to promote collaboration instead of hostility.

One further result of the deliverance of their message by the Elders may be justly described as a *call to do likewise.* Voices are needed to alert mankind so that it will forsake its cruel and selfishly motivated modes of living and replace them with kindness and gentleness toward all. Having heard the call, those who respond must accept personal responsibility for the welfare of everyone with whom they come in contact. This is perhaps one of the greatest opportunities that has ever existed; namely, having become illumined oneself, to share one's light with others, to reduce and ultimately cease from cruelty of all kinds; to call one's fellow human beings who are as yet not so moved to forsake the paths which produce pain, and tread one of gentleness, kindness and the avoidance of giving pain to any other sentient creature whatever. Such a change from an ignoble to a noble way of life, with its result of increased evolutionary progress for the individual who thus lives, leads to the reduction of suffering under karmic law from innumerable agencies, interior and external.

To bring home this truth to the human mind—that, no matter how different forms may appear, the Life of this universe is One Life—the Ancient Mysteries were founded and functioned at the heart of the great nations of the past. In the present era, selfishness and fear leading to wars, military and industrial, inevitably affect the rate of progress toward the restoration of the Ancient Mysteries as part of modern life. This delay, in its turn, increases the tragedy of our times and especially the tragic situation for those growing numbers of reincarnating Egos who seek again to live according to the Mystery Tradition. Restoration of the Mysteries in the present or near future in forms suitable to the time is, therefore, a pressing necessity. Without this aid, with its concomitant awakening within the human mind of realization of the divine Presence, immortal and eternal in every human being, wars of ever increasing destructiveness, cruelty, brutality, and crime will not only continue but increase in extent.

This Presence, as an indwelling spiritual Life, is one and the same in every human being. It is the essential attribute of man's whole nature and is also one and the same in every single person on earth. Full realization of the intimate interrelationship between man and man will bring the dawn of the Golden Age upon this darkened world period. Night with its nightmares will begin to give way to day, as the sunshine of wisdom revealing oneness dawns upon the human mind. Man's religion will then be based intellectually upon knowledge gained from a study of its own history. This will include the uttermost evil of selfishness—the figurative Satan—leading to cruelty and an acceptance, as the crowning virtue, of compassionate concern and love for every other sentient being in the human and the subhuman kingdoms. This, then, is the urgent and compulsory call to every idealist, to every human being who is experiencing an awakening to this knowledge and this ideal: "Let your own life shine forth as an example, and do all in your power, personally and through organized efforts to establish humaneness as the foundation-stone upon which the temple of the future will be built."

GLOSSARY

Adept (Latin). *Adeptus,* "He who has obtained." An initiate of the fifth degree in the Greater Mysteries, a Master in the science of esoteric philosophy, a perfected man, an exalted being who has attained complete mastery over his purely human nature and possesses knowledge and power commensurate with lofty evolutionary stature. A fully initiated being who watches over and guides the progress of humanity.

Ahamtāra (Sk.): The first tendency toward definiteness, regarded as the origin of all manifestation. In man the conception of "I," self-consciousness or self-identity, the illusion of self as a self-separate existence in contradistinction to the reality of the universal One Self. Awareness of this universality is expressed in the words of the Christ: "I and my Father are one." (John 10:30) The illusion of separateness, the "Great Heresy," is regarded as the source of human sorrow and suffering. Self-emancipation from this delusion is the sure way to happiness and peace.

Ātma (Sk.): The Self. The universal Spirit, the seventh principle in the septenary constitution of man, the supreme Soul. The Spirit-Essence of the universe. *(Paramātman*—" the Self Beyond.")

Aura (Gr. & Lat.): A subtle, invisible essence or fluid that emanates from human, animal, and even inanimate bodies. A psychic effluvium, superphysical and physical, including the electro-vital emanations from the physical body in the case of man. It is usually ovi-form or egg-shaped and is the seat of the Monadic, spiritual, intellectual, mental, passional, and vital energies, faculties, and potentialities of the whole sevenfold man.

210

Avatār (Sk.): The doctrine of Divine incarnation or "descent".

Buddhi (Sk.): The sixth principle of man, that of intuitive wisdom, vehicle of the seventh, *Atma,* the supreme soul in man. Universal soul. The faculty which manifests as spiritual intuitiveness. The bliss aspect of the Trinity.

Causal Body: The immortal body of the reincarnating Ego of man, built of matter of the "higher" levels of the mental world. It is called *Causal* because it gathers up within it the results of all experiences, and these act as causes molding future lives and influencing future conduct.

Chakra (Sk.): A "wheel" or "disc." A spinning, vortical, funnel-shaped force-center with its opening on the surfaces of the etheric and subtler bodies of man and its stem leading to the superphysical counterparts of the spinal cord and of nerve centers or glands. There are seven main chakras associated severally with the sacrum, the spleen, the solar plexus, the heart, the throat, and the pituitary and pineal glands. Chakras are both organs of superphysical consciousness and conveyors of the life-force between the superphysical and physical bodies. See *The Chakras,* C. W. Leadbeater.

God: In occult philosophy the term *God* in its highest meaning refers to a Supreme, Eternal, and Indefinable Reality. This Absolute is inconceivable, ineffable, and unknowable. Its revealed existence is postulated in three terms: an absolute existence, an absolute consciousness, and an absolute bliss. Infinite consciousness is regarded as inherent in the Supreme Being as a dynamic force that manifests the potentialities held in its own infinitude, and calls into being forms out of its own formless depths.

Gunas (Sk.): "A string or cord." The three qualities or attributes inherent in matter: *Rajas,* activity, desire; *Sattva,* harmony, rhythm; *Tamas,* inertia, stagnation. These correspond to the three aspects of the Trinity—Father, Son, and Holy Ghost, or Brahmā, in Vishnu, and Shiva, respectively.

Hierophant (Gr.): "One who explains sacred things." The discloser of sacred learning and the chief of the initiates. A title belonging to the highest Adepts in the temples of antiquity, who were teachers and expounders of the Mysteries and the initiators into the final great Mysteries.

Initiate: From the Latin *Initiatus.* The designation of anyone who was received into and had revealed to him the mysteries and secrets of occult philosophy.

211

Initiation: A profound spiritual and psychological regeneration, as a result of which a new "birth," a new beginning and a new life are entered upon. The word itself, from the Latin *Initia,* also implies the basic or first principles of any science, suggesting that initiates are consciously united with their own first principle, the Monad from which they emerged. Both the Lesser and the Greater Mysteries, ancient and modern, confer initiations of various degrees upon successful candidates.

Karma (Sk.): Action, connoting both the law of action and reaction, cause and effect, and the results of its operation upon nations and individuals. See *Reincarnation, Fact or Fallacy?*, Geoffrey Hodson.

Kundalini (Sk.): "The coiled up, universal Life Principle." A sevenfold, superphysical, occult power in universe and man, functioning in the latter by means of a spiral or coiling action, mainly in the spinal cord, but also throughout the nervous systems. It is represented in Greek symbology by the caduceus. When supernormally aroused this fiery force ascends into the brain by a serpentine path, hence its other name, the "Serpent Fire".

Logos (Gr.): The Word, "A divine, spiritual Entity". The manifested Deity, the outward expression or effect of the ever-concealed Cause. Thus speech is the *Logos* of thought, and *Logos* is correctly translated into Latin as *Verbum* and into English as *Word* in the metaphysical sense.

Monad (Gr.): "Alone." The divine spirit in man, the "Dweller in the Innermost", which is said to unfold through the subhuman kingdoms of nature into the human and thence to the stature of the Adept, beyond which extend unlimited evolutionary heights. The description of the destiny of man given by the Lord Christ supports this concept, for He said: "Be ye (Ye shall be—R. V.) therefore perfect, even as your Father which is in heaven is perfect." (Matt. 5:48—A. V.).

Nirvāna (Sk.): "Having life extinguished." Conscious absorption in the One Life of the cosmos, or absolute consciousness (Buddhism).

Occultist: A student of the "hidden" powers, forces, and intelligences in nature. While necromancy may—very undesirably—be resorted to by such a student, the practice is frowned upon by all teachers of white or wholly altruistic occultism. These point out that the discovery of truth demands increasing self-control, and that any surrender of one's will to another leads to self-delusion and untruth.

All researches motived by the twin ideals of attaining knowledge and so of becoming more helpful to mankind are, in consequence, carried out while in command of mind and will. The power to produce occult phenomena is developed by self-training, but these are always the result of the will and thought of the operator employed in full consciousness and complete self-command, which are essential to success.

Occult Science: "The science of the secrets of nature—physical and psychic, mental and spiritual; called Hermetic and Esoteric Sciences. In the West, the Kabbalah may be named; in the East, mysticism, magic, and Yoga philosophy, which latter is often referred to by the Chelas in India as the *seventh* Darshana (school of philosophy), there being only *six Darshanas* in India known to the world of the profane. These sciences are, and have been for ages, hidden from the vulgar for the very good reason that they would never be appreciated by the selfish educated classes, nor understood by the uneducated; whilst the former might misuse them for their own profit, and thus turn the divine science into *black magic*. . . ." q.v. *The Theosophical Glossary,* H. P. Blavatsky.

Skandhas (Sk.): "Groups of innate attributes" of the finite which endure between macrocosmic manifestations and microcosmic incarnation, uniting and reappearing as inherent qualities at the dawn of a new cycle of manifestation and at each human birth.

\

INDEX

OTHER AVAILABLE QUEST BOOKS

CREATIVE MEDITATION AND MULTI-DIMENSIONAL CONSCIOUSNESS
A bridge between the metaphysics of the East and West
by Lama Anagarika Govinda

CANDLE OF VISION
An autobiography of the great Irish mystic
by AE (George William Russell)

EXPANSION OF AWARENESS
One man's search for a meaning to life
by Arthur W. Osborn

GLORIOUS PRESENCE
The Vedanta philosophy including a translation of "Meditations on the South Facing Form."
by Ernest Wood

A HUMAN HERITAGE
Integrating scientific data and intuitional wisdom
by Alfred Taylor

LIGHT ON THE PATH
Aphorisms attributed to ancient Sanskrit work (in English)
by Mabel Collins

SILENT ENCOUNTER
Mysticism. Including essays by Haridas Chaudhuri, Geoffrey Hodson, Manley Hall.
Ed. by Virginia Hanson

VOICE OF THE SILENCE
Fragments from Book of the Golden Precepts
by Helena Petrovna Blavatsky

QUEST BOOKS
306 W. Geneva Road, Wheaton, Ill. 60187